The Communist Horizon

The Communist Horizon

JODI DEAN

VERSO
London • New York

First published by Verso 2012
© Jodi Dean 2012

The moral rights of the author have been asserted

1 3 5 7 9 10 8 6 4 2

Verso
UK: 6 Meard Street, London W1F 0EG
U.S.: 20 Jay Street, Suite 1010, Brooklyn, NY 11201

www.versobooks.com

Verso is the imprint of New Left Books
ISBN-13: 978-1-84467-954-6

British Library Cataloguing in Publication Data
A catalogue record for this book is available from the British Library

Library of Congress Cataloging-in-Publication Data
A catalog record for this book is available from the Library of Congress

Typeset in Bodoni by MJ Gavan, Truro, Cornwall
Printed in the US by Maple Vail

Contents

Introduction

The term "horizon" marks a division. Understood spatially, the horizon is the line dividing the visible, separating earth from sky. Understood temporally, the horizon converges with loss in a metaphor for privation and depletion. The "lost horizon" suggests abandoned projects, prior hopes that have now passed away. Astrophysics offers a thrilling, even uncanny, horizon: the "event horizon" surrounding a black hole. The event horizon is the boundary beyond which events cannot escape. Although "event horizon" denotes the curvature in space/time effected by a singularity, it's not much different from the spatial horizon. Both evoke a fundamental division that we experience as impossible to reach, and that we can neither escape nor cross.

I use "horizon" not to recall a forgotten future but to designate a dimension of experience that we can never lose, even if, lost in a fog or focused on our feet, we fail to see it. The horizon is Real in the sense of *impossible*—we can never reach it—and in the sense of *actual* (Jacques Lacan's notion of the Real includes both these senses). The horizon shapes our setting. We can lose our bearings, but the horizon is a necessary dimension of our actuality. Whether the effect of a singularity or the meeting of earth and sky, the horizon is the fundamental division establishing where we are.

With respect to politics, the horizon that conditions our experience is communism. I get the term "communist horizon" from Bruno Bosteels. In *The Actuality of Communism*, Bosteels engages with the work of Álvaro García Linera. García Linera ran as Evo Morales's vice presidential running mate in the Bolivian Movement for Socialism—Political Instrument for the Sovereignty of the Peoples (MAS-IPSP). He is the author of multiple pieces on Marxism, politics, and sociology, at least one of which was written while he served time in prison for promoting an armed uprising (before becoming vice president of Bolivia, he fought in the Tupac Katari Guerrilla Army). Bosteels quotes García Linera's response to an interviewer's questions about his party's plans following their electoral victory: "The general

horizon of the era is communist."[1] García Linera
doesn't explain the term. Rather, as Bosteels points
out, García Linera invokes the communist horizon "as
if it were the most natural thing in the world," as if
it were so obvious as to need neither explanation nor
justification. He assumes the communist horizon as an
irreducible feature of the political setting: "We enter
the movement with our expecting and desiring eyes
set upon the communist horizon." For García Linera,
communism conditions the actuality of politics.

Some on the Left dismiss the communist horizon as
a lost horizon. For example, in a postmodern plural-
ist approach that appeals to many on the Left, the
economists writing as J. K. Gibson-Graham reject
communism, offering "post-capitalism" in its stead.
They argue that descriptions of capitalism as a global
system miss the rich diversity of practices, relations,
and desires constituting yet exceeding the economy
and so advocate "reading the economy for difference
rather than dominance" (as if dominance neither

1   Bruno Bosteels, *The Actuality of Communism*, London:
Verso, 2011, 236.

presupposes nor relies on difference).[2] In their view, reading for difference opens up new possibilities for politics as it reveals previously unacknowledged loci of creative action within everyday economic activities.

Gibson-Graham do not present Marxism as a failed ideology or communism as the fossilized remainder of an historical experiment gone horribly wrong. On the contrary, they draw inspiration from Marx's appreciation of the social character of labor. They engage Jean-Luc Nancy's emphasis on communism as an idea that is the "index of a task of thought still and increasingly open."[3] They embrace the reclamation of the commons. And they are concerned with neoliberalism's naturalization of the economy as a force exceeding the capacity of people to steer or transform it.

Yet at the same time, Gibson-Graham push away from communism to launch their vision of post-capitalism. Communism is that against which they construct their alternative conception of the economy. It's a constitutive force, present as a shaping of the view they advocate. Even as Nancy's evocation of

2 J. K. Gibson-Graham, *A Post-Capitalist Politics*, Minneapolis, MN: University of Minnesota Press, 2006, 59.
3 Ibid., 82.

communism serves as a horizon for their thinking, they explicitly jettison the term "communism," which they position as the object of "widespread aversion" and which they associate with the "dangers of posing a positivity, a normative representation." Rejecting the positive notion of "communism," they opt for a term that suggests an empty relationality to the capitalist system they ostensibly deny, "post-capitalism." For Gibson-Graham, the term "capitalist" is not a term of critique or opprobrium; it's not part of a manifesto. The term is a cause of the political problems facing the contemporary Left. They argue that the *discursive* dominance of capitalism embeds the Left in paranoia, melancholia, and moralism.

Gibson-Graham's view is a specific instance of a general assumption shared by leftists who embrace a generic post-capitalism but eschew a more militant anticapitalism. Instead of actively opposing capitalism, this tendency redirects anticapitalist energies into efforts to open up discussions and find ethical spaces for decision—and this in a world where one bond trader can bring down a bank in a matter of minutes.

I take the opposite position. The dominance of capitalism, the capitalist *system*, is material. Rather than entrapping us in paranoid fantasy, an analysis that treats capitalism as a global system of appropriation, exploitation, and circulation that enriches the few as it dispossesses the many *and* that has to expend an enormous amount of energy in doing so can anger, incite, and galvanize. Historically, in theory and in practice, critical analysis of capitalist exploitation has been a powerful weapon in collective struggle. It persists as such today, in global acknowledgment of the excesses of neoliberal capitalism. As recently became clear in worldwide rioting, protest, and revolution, linking multiple sites of exploitation to narrow channels of privilege can replace melancholic fatalism with new assertions of will, desire, and collective strength. The problem of the Left hasn't been our adherence to a Marxist critique of capitalism. It's that we have lost sight of the communist horizon, a glimpse of which new political movements are starting to reveal.

Sometimes capitalists, conservatives, and liberal-democrats use a rhetoric that treats communism as a lost horizon. But usually they keep communism firmly within their sight. They see communism as a threat, twenty years after its ostensible demise. To them, communism is so threatening that they premise political

INTRODUCTION 7

discussion on the repression of the communist alternative. In response to left critiques of *democracy* for its failure to protect the interests of poor and working-class people, conservatives and liberals alike scold that "everybody knows" and "history shows" that *communism* doesn't work. Communism might be a nice ideal, they concede, but it always leads to violent, authoritarian excesses of power. They shift the discussion to communism, trying to establish the limits of reasonable debate. Their critique of communism establishes the political space and condition of democracy. Before the conversation even gets going, liberals, democrats, capitalists, and conservatives unite to block communism from consideration. It's off the table.

Those who suspect that the inclusion of liberals and democrats in a set with capitalists and conservatives is illegitimate are probably democrats themselves. To determine whether they belong in the set of those who fear communism, they should consider whether they think any evocation of communism should come with qualifications, apologies, and condemnations of past excesses. If the answer is "yes," then we have a clear indication that liberal democrats, and probably radical democrats as well, still consider communism a threat that must be suppressed—and so they belong in a set with capitalists and conservatives. All are anxious about the forces that communist desire risks unleashing.

There are good reasons for liberals, democrats, capitalists, and conservatives to be anxious. Over the last decade a return to communism has re-energized the Left. Communism is again becoming a discourse and vocabulary for the expression of universal, egalitarian, and revolutionary ideals. In March 2009, the Birkbeck Institute for the Humanities hosted a conference entitled "On the Idea of Communism." Initially planned for about 200 people, the conference ultimately attracted over 1,200, requiring a spillover room to accommodate those who couldn't fit in the primary auditorium. Since then, multiple conferences—in Paris, Berlin, and New York—and publications have followed, with contributions from such leading scholars as Alain Badiou, Étienne Balibar, Bruno Bosteels, Susan Buck-Morss, Costas Douzinas, Peter Hallward, Michael Hardt, Antonio Negri, Jacques Rancière, Alberto Toscano, and Slavoj Žižek.

The conferences and publications consolidate discussions that have been going on for decades. For over thirty years, Antonio Negri has sought to build a new approach to communism out of a Marxism reworked via Spinoza and the Italian political experiments of the 1970s. The *Empire* trilogy that Negri coauthored with Michael Hardt offers an affirmative, non-dialectical reconceptualization of labor, power, and the State, a new theory of communism from below. Alain Badiou has been occupied with communism for over forty years, from his philosophical and political engagement with Maoism, to his emphasis on the "communist invariants"—egalitarian justice, disciplinary terror, political volunteerism, and trust in the people—to his recent appeal to the communist Idea. Communism is not a new interest for Slavoj Žižek either. In early 2001 he put together a conference and subsequent volume rethinking Lenin. Where Negri and Badiou reject the Party and the State, Žižek retains a certain fidelity to Lenin. "The key 'Leninist' lesson today," he writes, is that "politics without the organizational form of the Party is politics without politics."[4] In short, a vital area of radical philosophy considers communism a contemporary name for emancipatory, egalitarian politics and

4 Slavoj Žižek, *Revolution at the Gates*, London: Verso, 2002, 297.

has been actively rethinking many of the concepts that form part of the communist legacy.

These ongoing theoretical discussions overlap with the changing political sequences marked by 1968 and 1989. They also overlap with the spread of neoliberal capitalist domination, a domination accompanied by extremes in economic inequality, ethnic hatred, and police violence, as well as by widespread militancy, insurgency, occupation, and revolution. The current emphasis on communism thus exceeds the coincidence of academic conferences calling specifically for communism's return with the new millennium's debt crises, austerity measures, increased unemployment, and overall sacrifice of the achievements of the modern welfare state to the private interests of financial institutions deemed too big to fail. Already in an interview in 2002, prior to his election to the Bolivian presidency, Evo Morales had announced that "the neoliberal system was a failure, and now it's the poor people's turn."[5] Communism is reemerging as a magnet of political energy because it is and has been the alternative to capitalism.

5   Evo Morales, "Interview with Evo Morales," Yvonne Zimmermann, *The Commoner*, July 7, 2002, commoner.org. uk/morales1.htm.

The communist horizon is not lost. It is Real. In this book, I explore some of the ways the communist horizon manifests itself to us today. As Bosteels argues, to invoke the communist horizon is to produce "a complete shift in perspective or a radical ideological turnabout, as a result of which capitalism no longer appears as the only game in town and we no longer have to be ashamed to set our expecting and desiring eyes here and now on a different organization of social relationships."[6] With communism as our horizon, the field of possibilities for revolutionary theory and practice starts to change shape. Barriers to action fall away. New potentials and challenges come to the fore. Anything is possible.

Instead of a politics thought primarily in terms of resistance, playful and momentary aesthetic disruptions, the immediate specificity of local projects, and struggles for hegemony within a capitalist parliamentary setting, the communist horizon impresses upon us the necessity to abolish capitalism and to create global practices and institutions of egalitarian cooperation. The shift in perspective the communist horizon

6 Bosteels, *The Actuality of Communism*, 228.

produces turns us away from the democratic milieu that has been the form of the loss of communism as a name for left aspiration and toward the reconfiguration of the components of political struggle—in other words, away from general inclusion, momentary calls for broad awareness, and lifestyle changes, and toward militant opposition, tight organizational forms (party, council, working group, cell), and the sovereignty of the people over the economy through which we produce and reproduce ourselves.

Some might object to my use of the second-person plural "we" and "us"—*what do you mean "we"?* This objection is symptomatic of the fragmentation that has pervaded the Left in Europe, the UK, and North America. Reducing invocations of "we" and "us" to sociological statements requiring a concrete, delineable, empirical referent, it erases the division necessary for politics as if interest and will were only and automatically attributes of a fixed social position. We-skepticism displaces the performative component of the second-person plural as it treats collectivity with suspicion and privileges a fantasy of individual singularity and autonomy. I write "we" hoping to enhance a partisan sense of collectivity. My break with conventions of writing that reinforce individualism by admonishing attempts to think and speak as part of a larger collective subject is deliberate.

The boundaries to what can be thought as politics in certain segments of the post-structuralist and anarchist Left only benefit capital. Some activists and theorists think that micropolitical activities, whether practices of self-cultivation or individual consumer choices, are more important loci of action than large-scale organized movement—an assumption which adds to the difficulty of building new types of organizations because it makes thinking in terms of collectivity rarer, harder, and seemingly less "fresh." Similarly, some activists and theorists treat aesthetic objects and creative works as displaying a political potentiality missing from classes, parties, and unions. This aesthetic focus disconnects politics from the organized struggle of working people, making politics into what spectators see. Artistic products, whether actual commodities or commodified experiences, thereby buttress capital as they circulate political affects while displacing political struggles from the streets to the galleries. Spectators can pay (or donate) to feel radical without having to get their hands dirty. The dominant class retains its position and the contradiction between this class and the rest of us doesn't make itself felt as such. The celebration of momentary actions and singular happenings—the playful disruption, the temporarily controversial film or novel—works the same way. Some on the anarchist and post-structuralist Left treat these flickers as the only proper instances of a contemporary left politics. A pointless action involving the momentary expenditure of enormous effort—the artistic equivalent of the 5k and 10k runs to fight cancer, that is to say, to increase awareness of cancer without actually doing much else—the singular happening disconnects task from goal. Any "sense" it makes, any meaning or relevance it has, is up to the spectator (perhaps with a bit of guidance from curators and theorists).

Occupation contrasts sharply with the singular happening. Even as specific occupations emerge from below rather than through a coordinated strategy, their common form—including its images, slogans, terms, and practices—links them together in a mass struggle.

The power of the return of communism stands or falls on its capacity to inspire large-scale organized collective struggle toward a goal. For over thirty years, the Left has eschewed such a goal, accepting instead liberal notions that goals are strictly individual life-style choices or social-democratic claims that history already solved basic problems of distribution with the compromise of regulated markets and welfare states—a solution the Right rejected and capitalism destroyed. The Left failed to defend a vision of a better world, an egalitarian world of common production by and for the collective people. Instead, it accommodated capital, succumbing to the lures of individualism, consumer-ism, competition, and privilege, and proceeding as if there really were no alternative to states that rule in the interests of markets.

Marx expressed the basic principle of the alterna-tive over a hundred years ago: from each according to ability, to each according to need. This principle con-tains the urgency of the struggle for its own realization. We don't have to continue to live in the wake of left failure, stuck in the repetitions of crises and specta-cle. In light of the planetary climate disaster and the ever-intensifying global class war as states redistrib-ute wealth to the rich in the name of austerity, the absence of a common goal is the absence of a future (other than the ones imagined in post-apocalyptic sce-narios like *Mad Max*). The premise of communism is that collective determination of collective conditions is possible, if we want it.

To help incite this desire, to add to its reawakening force and presence, I treat "communism" as a tag for six features of our current setting:

1. A specific image of the Soviet Union and its collapse;
2. A present, increasingly powerful force;
3. The sovereignty of the people;
4. The common and the commons;
5. The egalitarian and universalist desire that cuts through the circuits and practices in which we are trapped;
6. The party.

The first two features can be loosely associated with the politics that configures itself via a history linked to the end of the Soviet Union as a state, as refracted through the dominance of the US as a state. What matters here is less the historical narrative than the expression of communism as the force of an absence. My discussion of these first two features highlights how the absence of communism shapes our contemporary setting.

In the sequence narrated as the triumph of capitalism

and liberal democracy, the communist horizon makes itself felt as a "signifying stress." This is Eric L. Santner's term for a way that reality expresses its non-identity with itself. As Santner explains, the "social formation in which we find ourselves immersed" is "fissured by lack" and "permeated by inconsistency and incompleteness." The lack calls out to us. Inconsistency and incompleteness make themselves felt. "What is registered," Santner explains, "are not so much forgotten deeds but forgotten failures to act."[7] The frenetic activity of contemporary communicative capitalism deflects us away from these gaps. New entertainments, unshakeable burdens, and growing debt displace our attention toward the immediate and the coming-up-next as they attempt to drown out the forceful effects of the unrealized—the unrealized potentials of unions and collective struggle, the unrealized claims for equality distorted by a culture that celebrates the excesses of the very rich, the unrealized achievements of collective solidarity in redressing poverty and redistributing risks and rewards. The first two chapters thus

7 Eric L. Santner, "Miracles Happen," in *The Neighbor*, Slavoj Žižek, Eric L. Santner, Kenneth Reinhard, Chicago: University of Chicago Press, 2005, 85–89.

treat the gaps, fissures, and lack Santner theorizes as signifying stresses in terms of a missing communism that makes itself felt in the setting configured by its alleged failure and defeat.

The second two features of the present that communism tags are positive (rather than present as the force of the unrealized or absent): the people in their common political and economic activity. In these chapters, I grapple with the question of class struggle today. If Hardt and Negri are right (and I think they are) to argue that "communication is the form of capitalist production in which capital has succeeded in submitting society entirely and globally to its regime" (I use the term "communicative capitalism" to bring out this amplified role of communication in production), what are the repercussions for understanding class struggle? Does it make sense to continue to emphasize the proletariat? I argue that it does not, not if by "proletariat" one has in mind an empirical social class. More useful is the idea of proletarianization as a process of exploitation, dispossession, and immiseration that produces the very rich as the privileged class that lives off the rest of us. I offer the notion of "the people as the rest of us," the people as a divided and divisive force, as an alternative to some of the other names for the subject of communism—proletariat, multitude, part-of-no-part.

How the people divide or how the non-coincidence of the people is inflected and qualified is a matter of politics. Political organizations respond to this division, construing and directing it in one way rather than another. Accordingly, I end this book by taking up the question of the communist party. Although actively calling for the reclamation of communism as the name for a revolutionary universal egalitarianism, Badiou insists on a communism disconnected from the "outmoded" forms of Party and State. Hardt and Negri likewise reject Party and State: *"Being communist means being against the State."*[8] They emphasize instead the constituent power of desire and the affective, creative productivity of the multitude as the communism underpinning and exceeding capitalism. This is not my view. I agree with Bosteels and Žižek that a politics without the organizational form of the party is a politics without politics.

Conceptualizing the party of communists in our

8 Antonio Negri, "Communism: Some Thoughts on the Concept and Practice," in *The Idea of Communism*, ed. Costas Douzinas and Slavoj Žižek, London: Verso, 2010, 158.

contemporary setting is and must be an ongoing project. As Bosteels argues, "party" does not name an instrument for carrying out the iron laws of history but "the flexible organization of a fidelity to events in the midst of unforeseeable circumstances."[9] I'm tempted to use terms from complexity theory here: the party is a complex, adaptive system. Its end is proletarian revolution, that is, the destruction of the capitalist system of exploitation and expropriation, of *proletarianization*, and the creation of a mode of production and distribution where the free development of each is compatible with the free development of all. We don't yet know how we will structure our communist party—in part because we stopped thinking about it, giving way instead to the transience of issues, ease of one-click networked politics, and the illusion that our individual activities would immanently converge in a plurality of post-capitalist practices of creating and sharing. But we know that we need to find a mode of struggle that can scale, endure, and cultivate the collective desire for collectivity. And we know that we can learn from the past and are learning from ongoing experiments in

9   Bosteels, *The Actuality of Communism*, 243.

organization. I thus conclude by considering how occupation is or is becoming such an organizational form, a political form for the incompatibility between capitalism and the people.

The communist horizon appears closer than it has in a long time. The illusion that capitalism works has been shattered by all manner of economic and financial disaster—and we see it everywhere. The fantasy that democracy exerts a force for economic justice has dissolved as the US government funnels trillions of dollars to banks and the European central banks rig national governments and cut social programs in order to keep themselves afloat. With our desiring eyes set on the communist horizon, we can now get to work on collectively shaping a world that we already make in common.

Chapter One

Our Soviets

For people in the United States, the most conventional referent of communism is the Soviet Union. Displaced by four decades of Cold War, a war that shaped US-American policies and identities, aspirations and fears, the multiplicity of historical and theoretical communisms condense into one—the USSR.[1] Rather than changing over time, including the international range of parties and movements, or acknowledging active communist movement in the US, communism is one, and this one is fixed as the USSR.

To make this referent explicit, though, leads to complications.

The USSR was never fixed or one. The unity imposed on it by the Cold War binary is false, undermined by

1 Susan Buck-Morss demonstrates how the structuring logic of the Cold War was already in place by the end of World War I. See her *Dreamworld and Catastrophe*, Cambridge, MA: MIT Press, 2000.

the actual historical relationship between the Soviet Union and the United States. This relationship disturbs the easy equation of communism with the USSR insofar as communism becomes an element of US self-identity. The two regimes, sometimes allies and sometimes enemies, were deeply interconnected. They were symbolically identified in that each provided the other with a standpoint from which to see and evaluate itself. Each reminded the other of its failure and potential. Seeing themselves from the standpoint of the other, they made the other a component of their understanding of themselves.

Imagining itself in the eyes of the Soviets, the US never seemed equal enough. Segregation, Jim Crow, and severe poverty appeared all the more shameful when put in relief against the Soviet system's project of collective ownership and avowal of equality. Our biggest rival seemed to be doing better by its citizens than we were doing by ours. A key impulse to progress in civil rights and social welfare, then, stemmed from the US government's desire not to look bad when compared to the USSR.

The distorted US treatment of consumer items as markers of equality resulted from this same structure

—capitalist excess came to be not merely justified
in the name of democracy but the very definition of
it. Susan Buck-Morss describes the "parable of the
Democracy of Goods" that advertisers proffered and
the US government supported. She writes, "The United
States government joined the capitalist class in its ideological commitment to the expansion of consumption
without limits. Similarities of consumer styles came
to be viewed as synonymous with social equality, and
not merely as a compensation for its lack. Democracy
was freedom of consumer choice. To suggest otherwise was un-American."[2] Who was the merging of
consumer goods and democracy for? Not Americans.
US-Americans have long valued individual freedom
more than democracy. We didn't need some kind of
compensation for the inequity and inadequacy of capitalist democracy. Consumer goods are attractive and
pleasurable enough on their own without the ideological element; they don't need a democratic supplement.
The treatment of consumer goods as markers of equality and indicators of democracy was for the Soviet other
before whose judging gaze the US imagined itself.

2   Ibid., 204.

Whose citizens were better off? Symbolic identification with the USSR made the US consider this question in terms of equality. Anxiety over equality animated American ridicule of communist laziness and lack of private property, of the unbearable uniformity of Soviet ways of life, and of the emptiness of the store shelves and the unending lines. Highlighting the wealth of the few, the US obscured the poverty of many of its citizens. At the same time, it attempted to evade its own concerns with its shallowness as a society, its tendencies to allow consumerism and private life to substitute for grand struggles and ideals. Viewing itself from the Soviet perspective, the US saw itself as lacking, as failing to secure for its own citizens what communism secured for Soviet citizens.

From the US perspective (as imagined by the Soviets) the measure of communist success depended on productivity. Who was all the heavy industry for? Before which gaze is it imagined? Not the suffering Soviet people. Rather, the gaze was American. One need only recall the Soviet goal of "catching up and overtaking" the West. Buck-Morss notes how the fantasy of productivity, opened up by symbolic identification with the US as über-producer, structured Soviet art and culture as well as politics and economics. Poets and artists celebrated machinery. Films and novels were devoted to steel production and the construction of factories. Precisely because the Soviet Union adopted "the capitalist heavy-industry definition of economic modernization," socialism remained caught within a very specific capitalist model of economic development. The Soviets did not reconstruct American capitalism. They glorified it. (Indeed, for some Soviets, Henry Ford was as close to a saint as one could get.[3])

The (reciprocal) symbolic identification of the US and the USSR shaped their senses of who and what they were such that democracy could morph into commodity consumption and production could become a utopia in and for itself. The real divisions of class and race in the US as well as of ethnicity and privilege in the USSR could sometimes be covered over by the ideals of productivity and equality for which each was admired. The US may not be equitable, but it is productive. The USSR may not have been productive, but it was equitable. Imagining themselves before the gaze of the other, they secured—for a time—fantasies

3   Ibid., 110.

of unity that depended on the repression of their identification with the ideology of the other.

The place of communism within the self-understanding of the US is not the only complication that arises when we begin to question and specify the referent of communism. The differences among parties, places, factions, and times that the unifying imaginary of Cold War communism tries to suppress also start to leak back into the history of Soviet communism. For example, the Soviet Union did not claim to have achieved communism, although its ruling party called itself a communist party. As is the case with any party or political system, the Communist Party in the Soviet Union changed over time, most drastically by moving from a revolutionary party to a governing bureaucratic party. As a governing body the Party experienced further changes, changes that were sometimes violent, sometimes incremental, often paid for with the lives of Party members themselves. Insofar as it was a political party, and for most of its history the only recognized political party, the Communist Party in the former Soviet Union was a locus of struggle and disagreement over a host of issues from art, literature, and science to economic development, foreign policy, and internal relations among the various republics. To be sure, efforts were made to present a unified front, to downplay the presence of disagreements within the Party. Yet a significant effect of these efforts was the amplification of ostensibly superficial differences: small divergences became signs of deeper conflict. Soviet citizens, allies, and enemies alike learned to discern in the distinction between a "frank" and a "comradely" exchange of opinions major shifts in political direction. In short, the Soviet Union isn't a very stable referent of communism.

US-Americans don't worry about that very much.

US-Americans are sheltered from anxiety over wobbly reference by the (fantastic) stability accompanying the proper name "Stalin." A legacy of the Cold War more than of critical inquiry into Soviet history, "Stalinist" tags practices of monopolizing and consolidating power in the Soviet party-state bureaucracy. In this circumscribed imaginary, communism as Stalinism is linked to authoritarianism, prison camps, and the inadmissibility of criticism. Just as communism as the Soviet Union overshadows a wide array of other communisms—from China, through Yugoslavia, to Cuba and Nepal, to the US, UK, and Europe, and from

parties coexisting within parliamentary state formations to revolutionary fighters operating under various
names and in various degrees of legitimacy—so does
the Soviet Union as Stalinism eclipse post-Stalinist
developments in the Soviet Union, particularly with
regard to successes in modernizing (including a highly
successful space program) and improving overall
standards of living. Tariq Ali quotes the Soviet dis-
sident Zhores Medvedev writing in 1979: "There is
no unemployment, but on the contrary a shortage of
labour—which creates a greater variety of job-choice
for workers. The average working family can easily
satisfy its immediate material needs: apartment,
stable employment, education for children, health
care, and so on. The prices of essential goods—bread,
milk, meat, fish, rent—have not changed since 1964.
The cost of television or radio sets and other durable
items has actually been reduced (from unduly high
previous levels)."[4] The US didn't and doesn't see the
Soviet Union this way. Blinkered by the Cold War,
it has remained fixated on a static image of grey
oppression.

4   Tariq Ali, *The Idea of Communism*, London: Seagull
Books, 2009, 81–82.

Against the background of communist = Soviet = Stalinist, two interlocking stories of the collapse of communism predominate. The first is that communism collapsed under its own weight: it was so inefficient, people were so miserable, life was so stagnant, that the system came to a grinding halt. It failed. Linked to Stalinism, the story of failure features chapters on famine, purges, and terror. Like most ideological constructions, it's not quite coherent: it neglects the fact that the Stalin period was also a period in which the US and USSR were allies. In the era most exemplary of the Soviet Union's injustice and illegitimacy, the period when the USSR was present not as a failed state but a strong one, the US was closer to the regime than at any other time in its history. The second, related, story of the collapse of communism is that it was defeated. We beat them. We won. Capitalism and liberal democracy (the elision is necessary) demonstrated their superiority on the world historical stage. Freedom triumphed over tyranny. The details of this victory matter less than its ostensible undeniability. After all, there is no Soviet Union anymore.

*   *   *

The chain communism-Soviet Union-Stalinism-collapse
sets the parameters for the appeal to history that is
characteristic of liberal, democratic, capitalist, and conservative attempts to repress the communist alternative.
Responding to challenges regarding the exclusion of
class struggle, proletarian revolution, collective ownership of the means of production, and the smashing of the
bourgeois-democratic state from political theory, they
invoke history as their ground and proof. History shows
that the communist project is a dead end. Yet as Alain
Badiou reminds us, "at bottom, it is always in the interests of the powerful that history is mistaken for politics,
that is, the objective is taken for the subjective."[5] What,
then, are the features of this invocation of history?

The first is objectivity. The product of a neutral,
unbiased investigation, the history of communism is
made to stand apart from the politics and struggles that
comprise this history, as if it were but a collection of
facts, information to be googled and accessed. These
facts are specifiable points or objects, immune to interpretation, and impossible to dispute.

If we accept, for a moment, the possibility of such

5   Alain Badiou, *Theory of the Subject*, trans. Bruno
Bosteels, London: Continuum, 2009, 44.

facts, and agree that they are crucial to our capacities to learn from previous struggles for communism, where will we find them? Michael E. Brown and Randy Martin argue persuasively that there is not yet a credible and established body of historical literature on communism, socialism, or the Soviet Union. Most of the histories we have were produced in the context of a hegemonic anticommunism.[6] Brown and Martin point out that the methodological and conceptual defects in scholarly studies of the Soviet Union would have been scandalous in other academic fields. Since the field was primarily a propaganda apparatus for the foreign policy establishment, these defects seemed somehow without significance, with the result, for example, that it is still impossible to say which aspects of the Soviet system were intrinsic to it and which resulted from external pressures, or, to take another example, whether the Soviet Union was a completely distinct and unique state formation or instead shared attributes with the United States or Nazi Germany that make communism a subset of a larger totalitarianism. In

6   This is not to say that there are no serious and significant works. One of the most impressive is Lars T. Lih, *Lenin Rediscovered*, Chicago, IL: Haymarket Books, 2008.

short, the effects of pervasive anticommunism continue
to outlive the Soviet Union. Brown and Martin write,
"The Communist icon of the Cold War is now the negative ideal type against which an absolutely idealized
capitalist market is both taken to be real and deemed
the only sustainable paradigm for universal human
organization."[7] Constituted out of the chain communism-Soviet Union-Stalinism-collapse, the invocation
of history reinforces a Cold War binary instead of highlighting the challenges facing an organized society of
producers.

A second feature of the history invoked to repress
the communist alternative is its continuity and
determinacy. Faced with an opponent who presents
communism as a solution to the crises of capitalism,
the invoker of history posits a necessary sequence, as if
revolutions were shielded from contingency. He starts
with a fact, a unique, specifiable object, and builds from
the fact a series of consequences and effects. These
consequences and effects are necessary and unavoidable: *if Lenin, then Stalin; if revolution, then gulag;*

7   Michael E. Brown and Randy Martin, "Left Futures,"
in Michael E. Brown, *The Historiography of Communism*,
Philadelphia, PA: Temple University Press, 2009, 177.

if Party, then purges. So even as some who appeal to history recognize the defects and dilemmas traversing the academic field, they nonetheless highlight specific facts and moments, perhaps from their own experience of betrayal in the compromises made by specific communist parties working in parliamentary contexts (as in France and Italy), as if these specific facts and moments were themselves indications of sequences of effects impossible to avoid. If it happened once, it will happen again, and there is nothing we can do about it. The oddity of this position is that communism is unique in its determining capacity, the one political arrangement capable of eliminating contingency and directing action along a singular vector. Communism becomes the exception to the dynamic of production, struggle, and experience that gives rise to it. Instead of the politics of a militant subject, communism is again an imaginary, immutable object, this time a linear process with a certain end.

As a consequence, history loses its own historicity. This is the third feature of the history invoked to repress the communist alternative. In this formation, history functions as a structure and a constant incapable of change and impenetrable by "external" forces.

Any particular moment is thus a container for this essential whole—the Leninist party, the Stalinist show trials, the KGB, the Brezhnev-era stagnation. Each is interchangeable with the other as an example of the error of communism precisely because communism is invariant. In contrast with capitalism's permanent revolution, historical communism appears as impossibly static. Only by supposing such an impossible, invariant, constant, unchanging communism can the appeal to history turn a single instance into a damning example of the failed and dangerous communist experience. And as it does, it disconnects communism from the very history to which it appeals, erasing not only communism as capitalism's self-critique but also communism as capitalism's mirror, ally, enemy, and Other.

Here, then, is the inner truth of the liberal, democratic, capitalist, and conservative appeal to history. The intent is not to inspire inquiry or stimulate new scholarly research. Rather, it is to preserve the fantasy that capitalism and democracy are the best possible economic and political arrangements. Excising communism from its history as the class struggle within capitalism, as the critique and revolution to which capitalism gives rise, this history without historicity derides communism for a necessity that it effectively reinstalls in a capitalism without alternatives.

The supposition of an eternal communism is not only the paradoxical effect of the attempt to derail the return of communism by appealing to a history seemingly immunized from change. Some at the forefront of communism's return likewise make recourse to a communism that transcends history. Badiou treats history as the purview of the State and communism as an eternal political idea. Bruno Bosteels acknowledges the tactical benefit of such a move: "Given the depoliticizing effects of the call constantly to historicize, not to mention the even more damning effects of the invocation of some figure or other of the world-historical tribunal, it can indeed be argued that history in and of itself no longer possesses the emancipatory power it once had."[8] Nonetheless, Bosteels urges that tactical ahistoricism be dialectically conjoined with a new writing of history, a new history of popular insurrection that recalls the wide range of struggles and movements communism names. Rather than joining Badiou

8   Bruno Bosteels, *The Actuality of Communism*, London: Verso, 2011, 277.

in sheltering communism in a philosophical Idea, Bosteels holds out the actuality of a communist politics that does not hypostasize past failures into permanent barriers to theorizing, organizing, and occupying party and state.

The best response to the appeal to history is to shatter the chain communism-Soviet Union-Stalinism-collapse and make a new one out of the rich variety of movements and struggles. This is a history of courage, revolt, and solidarity. It is also set in a communist present. If the end of the Soviet Union were the same as the end of communism, if 1991 marked a temporal horizon separating the validity of the Soviet experiment from the capitalist, liberal, democratic present, then communism would be past—like the Byzantine Empire. As a particular party-state formation, it would be an artifact to be analyzed and studied. Whatever gave it breath, made it real, would be gone. It would be a dead political language.

Yet communism persists. It is frequently evoked as a living presence or possibility, particularly in our current setting of global revolution and neoliberal crisis.

Chapter Two

Present Force

When the Soviet Union is the referent of communism, communism is thought as the descriptor of a specific political-economic arrangement. The adjective "communist" qualifies the noun of a party and/or a state. In the twenty-first century, Russia, Poland, Hungary, the Czech Republic and other countries previously part of the Soviet bloc tend to be referred to as "post-Soviet" rather than as "new-capitalist." For a while, particularly during the early years of forced privatization, the term "Mafioso capitalism" was heard a lot. Since the turn of the millennium, it has dropped from use. "Mafioso capitalism" hits too close to home, more fitting as a designator of neoliberalism's brutal, extreme, winner-take-all version of capitalism than of the temporary shock treatment involved in the transition out of state socialism.

For a variety of groups and ideological persuasions, communism still names the alternative to the

extreme inequality, insecurity, and racist, nationalist
ethnocentricism accompanying globalized neoliberal
capitalism. In the contemporary United States, "communist" exceeds the specificity of its adjectival confines
to serve as a term of opprobrium. One would think the
Cold War never ended. Sometimes communism blends
in with socialism. Other times it's conjoined to fascism.
(Too few Americans know the difference, a result of
the ideological effects of the notion of totalitarianism
as much as it is of a more general educational deficit.)

What is communist? National healthcare. Environ-
mentalism. Feminism. Public education. Collective
bargaining. Progressive taxation. Paid vacation days.
Gun control. The movement around Occupy Wall
Street. Bicycles are a "gateway drug" to communism.
Web 2.0 is communist because it holds out "the seduc-
tive promise of individual self-realization" that Karl
Marx evoked in "The German Ideology."[1]

Who is communist? Anyone who protested US
military aggression in Iraq and Afghanistan. Anyone
critical of the Bush administration. Anyone who wants
to tax the rich, close corporate tax loopholes, and

1   Andrew Keen, "Web 2.0," *The Weekly Standard*, February
14, 2006, weeklystandard.com.

regulate the derivatives market. Anyone who supports unemployment insurance, food stamps, public education, and public sector workers' rights to collective bargaining.

US President Barack Obama is labeled a communist —not to mention a Muslim, a Kenyan, and a terrorist. In January 2010, Victoria Jackson, a former cast member on the television show *Saturday Night Live*, released a video on YouTube called "There's a Communist Living in the White House." In April, Jackson performed the song at a Tea Party rally, where attendees joined in singing the chorus: "There's a communist living in the White House." Extensive commentary in the circuit of blogs, talk radio, and cable news followed, extending the "communist President" meme. Two years later, Florida Congressman Allen West alleged that as many as eighty members of the US House of Representatives were communists—he was referring to Democratic Party members of the Progressive Caucus.

It's obvious enough that contemporary Democrats are not communists. Most support policies to the right of Ronald Reagan's. The Democratic Party did not attempt to pass a single-payer public health insurance program (instead, people are required to purchase insurance from a private company). The Obama administration's response to the economic crisis of 2008 focused on the finance sector (when it could have provided a massive jobs program). President Obama himself introduced the possibility of cuts to the last remaining components of the welfare state—Social Security, Medicare, and Medicaid (all enormously popular programs). Evocations of an encroaching communist threat in the US could thus seem to be a not very creative return to the language of the Cold War and the Red Scare, a conservative retreat to a formerly effective rhetoric of fear.

Yet there is more to these evocations of communism than simply the dusting off of an old conflict. Gestures to communism and socialism make sense because the markets failed. When the US government bailed out the finance sector, the visibility of the state as an instrument of class power became undeniable. Of course, states have always been instruments of class power (that's what states are). And the corporate and financial elite in the United States have long used the state to secure their particular interests (most recently by subverting unions, manipulating the tax code, avoiding regulation, and structuring competition to benefit themselves). But the bank bailouts shattered any remaining illusion that the democratic state serves and represents the people. They demonstrated in a spectacular and irrefutable fashion that the government intervenes in the economy and does so on behalf of a class.

The next move is conceptually easy: use the state for a different class; use it to destroy the conditions that create classes. Since this is the definition of the dictatorship of the proletariat, it's no surprise that capitalists and conservatives evoke the threat of communism. The myth that the state has no role in the economy doesn't convince anyone. The bailouts proved the possibility and necessity of using the state for the common interest of the collective people.

Also contributing to the climate wherein communism is a present threat is a meme that doesn't use the word "communist" but focuses instead on the people as the source of excesses that must be eliminated or controlled. Conservative and mainstream media in the US, UK, and Europe blame the people for the debt and economic crises, and hence position cuts and austerity measures as the only viable solutions. In the US, the collapse in the derivatives and mortgage bond markets is attributed to poor people who took out mortgages they couldn't afford, defaulted on them, and thereby caused global economic chaos. Likewise, the demands of public sector workers—such as teachers, civil servants, police, and firefighters—for job security, pensions, benefits, decent wages, and the right to bargain collectively are said to be unaffordable. In the UK, the rights of working class students to an education are presented as beyond the country's means. Anyone who wants an education should be willing to pay for it. The Greek story is of people who refused to work enough, who wanted to retire early. Various capitalist governments tell the same story: the people's excesses are the problem and the solution is to beat them back into submission.

The truth in this story of the people, a story that erases its own telling as a salvo in class war—that is, as a tactic used by the state as an instrument of the very rich in their efforts to extract every crumb of value from working people—is that the people are a political and an economic cause. The welfare states of Europe and the Keynesian arrangements in the US and the UK resulted from political struggle. They were achievements of the organized collective power of working people. Workers fought for wages, benefits, pensions, a measure of control over their conditions of employment. Workers made demands and for over thirty years, capital had to pay. Capital didn't restrain itself. The people disciplined capital. The rhetoric of "we can't afford it," of deficits and cuts, of austerity and unpayable debts and all the rest, is the way capital expresses its refusal to pay anymore. Defaulting on loans is a problem more for lenders than for borrowers (a point that tends to remain hidden). Capital wants more and is demanding more—accumulation by dispossession.

One additional truth in the story that blames the people and in so doing treats them as a political and economic cause centers on the people's demands. Yet because this story is capital's story, it is inverted, backwards. The problem *is* with the people's demands, but not that we've demanded too much. It's the opposite: we've demanded too little. We haven't been demanding enough. We haven't followed up, refused, smashed, and taken more. The capitalist story presents precisely such a demanding, refusing, taking people. These are the people—a strong, massive, motley people—who the rich and their political agents talk as if they are fighting and who they target with excessive force at the slightest provocation (as the London riots in August

2011 made vividly clear, and as the tear gas and rubber bullets deployed by police in US cities against occupiers showed the following fall). These are the people they fear—the communist threat.

Slavoj Žižek argues that the ruling ideology wants us to think that radical change is impossible. This ideology, he says, tells us that it's impossible to abolish capitalism. Perpetually repeating its message of no alternative, the dominant ideology attempts to "render invisible the impossible-real of the antagonism that cuts across capitalist societies."[2] Žižek's description might have worked a decade or so ago, but not anymore. The end of the first decade of the twenty-first century has brought with it massive uprisings, demonstrations, strikes, occupations, and revolutions throughout the Middle East, EU, UK, and US. In the US, mainstream media remind viewers daily that radical change is possible, and incite us to fear it. The Right, even the center, regularly invokes the possibility of radical change, and it associates that change with communism.

Why communism? Because the gross inequality ushered in by the extreme capitalism of neoliberal state

2   Slavoj Žižek, "A Permanent Economic Emergency," *New Left Review* 65, July–August 2010, 94.

policy and desperate financialism is visible, undeniable, and global. Increasing in industrialized countries over the last three decades, income inequality is particularly severe in Chile, Mexico, Turkey, and the US, the four industrialized countries with the largest income gaps (Portugal, the UK, and Italy also make the top ten).[3] Inequality in the US is so extreme that its Gini coefficient (45) makes it more comparable to Cameroon (44.6) and Jamaica (45.5) than to Germany (30.4) and the UK (34).[4] The antagonism that cuts across capitalist countries is so apparent that dominant ideological forces can't obscure it.

The US typically positions extreme inequality, indebtedness, and decay elsewhere, offshore. The severe global economic recession, collapse in the housing and mortgage markets, increase in permanent involuntary unemployment, trillion-dollar bank bailouts, and extensive cuts to federal, state, and local

3   Organization for Economic Co-operation and Development, *Society at a Glance 2011—OECD Social Indicators*, April 2011, oecd.org.
4   Central Intelligence Agency, "Country Comparison: Distribution of Family Income—The Gini Index," *The World Factbook*, cia.gov.

budgets, however, have made what we thought was the
third world into *our world*. Contra Žižek, the division
cutting across capitalist societies is *more visible*, *more
palpable* in the US and UK *now* than it's been since at
least the 1920s. We learn that more of our children live
in poverty than at any time in recent history (20 percent
of children in the US as of 2010), that the wealth of the
very, very rich—the top 1 percent—has dramatically
increased while income for the rest of us has remained
stagnant or declined, that many of the foreclosures the
banks force on homeowners are meaningless, illegal
acts of expropriation (the banks can't document who
owns what so they lack the paper necessary to justify
foreclosure proceedings). We read of corporations
sitting on piles of cash instead of hiring back their laid-
off workforce. Under neoliberalism, they lavishly enjoy
their profits rather than put them back into production
—what Gérard Duménil and Dominique Lévy call an
explicit strategy of "disaccumulation."[5]

In fact, we read that the middle class is basically
finished. *Ad Age*, the primary trade journal for the

5 Gérard Duménil and Dominique Lévy, *The Crisis of
Neoliberalism*, Cambridge, MA: Harvard University Press,
2011, 64.

advertising industry, published a major report declaring the end of mass affluence. As if it were describing an emerging confrontation between two great hostile classes, the report notes the stagnation of working class income and the exponential growth of upper class income: most consumer spending comes from the top 10 percent of households. For advertisers, the only consumers worth reaching are the "small plutocracy of wealthy elites" with "outsize purchasing influence," an influence that creates "an increasingly concentrated market in luxury goods."[6]

Admittedly, popular media in the US rarely refer to the super rich as the bourgeoisie and the rest of us as the proletariat. They are more likely to use terms like "Wall Street" versus "Main Street"—which is one of the reasons Occupy Wall Street took hold as a movement; people were already accustomed to hearing about all that had been done to save the banks. Sometimes, US popular media avoids a direct contrast between the 1 percent and the 99 percent, instead juxtaposing executive pay with strapped consumers looking for bargains

6 Sam Pizzigati, "Madison Avenue Declares 'Mass Affluence' Over," *Campaign for America's Future*, May 30, 2011, ourfuture.org.

or cutting back on spending. In 2010, median pay for the top executives increased 23 percent; the CEO of Viacom, Philippe P. Dauman, made 84.5 million dollars.[7] CEOs from top banks enjoyed a 36 percent increase, with Jamie Dimon from JP Morgan Chase and Lloyd Blankfein from Goldman Sachs topping the list.[8] Even CEOs of companies experiencing major losses and declines have been getting extreme bonuses: General Electric's CEO, Jeffrey R. Immelt, received an average of 12 million dollars a year over a six-year period while the company had a 7 percent decline in returns; Gregg L. Engles, CEO of Dean Foods, took away an average of 20.4 million dollars a year over six years while the company declined 11 percent.[9] Super high pay doesn't reward performance. It's a form of theft through which the very rich serve themselves, bestowing a largesse that keeps money within their class.

In a setting like the US where the mantra for over fifty years has been "what's good for business is good

7   Pradnya Joshi, "We Knew They Got Raises. But This?" *New York Times*, July 2, 2011, nytimes.com.

8   Megan Murphy and Sharlene Goff, "Bank Chiefs Average Pay Rises by 36 Percent," *Financial Times*, June 15, 2011, cnbc.com.

9   "In Pictures: Worst Bosses For The Buck," forbes.com.

for America," the current undeniability of division
is significant. Inequality is appearing as a factor, a
force, even a crime. Every sector of US society views
class conflict as the primary conflict in the country.[10]
No wonder we are hearing the name "communism"
again—the antagonism cutting across capitalist societies is palpable, pressing.

The Right positions communism as a threat because
communism names the defeat of and alternative to
capitalism. It recognizes the crisis in capitalism: overaccumulation leaves the rich sitting on piles of cash
they can't invest; industrial capacity remains unused
and workers remain unemployed; global interconnec-
tions make unneeded skyscrapers, fiber-optic cables,
malls, and housing developments as much a part of
China as the US. At the same time, scores of significant
problems—whether linked to food shortages resulting
from climate change, energy shortages resulting from oil
dependency, or drug shortages resulting from the failure
of private pharmaceutical companies to risk their own
capital—remain unmet because they require the kinds

10   Rich Morin, "Rising Share of Americans See Conflict
Between Rich and Poor," *Pew Research Center*, January 11,
2012, pewsocialtrends.org.

of large-scale planning and cooperation that capitalism, particularly in its contemporary finance- and communications-driven incarnation, subverts. David Harvey explains that capitalists these days construe a healthy economy as one that grows about 3 percent a year. The likelihood of continued 3 percent annual growth in the world economy, however, is small. This is in part because of the difficulty of reabsorbing surplus capital. By 2030 it would be necessary to find investment opportunities for three trillion dollars, roughly twice what was needed in 2010.[11] The future of capitalism is thus highly uncertain—and, for capitalists, grim.

Neoliberals and neoconservatives evoke the threat of communism because they sense the mortality of capitalism. We shouldn't let the media screen deceive us. We shouldn't think that the charge that Obama is a communist and peace is communist fool us into thinking that communism is just an image covering up and distorting the more serious politics of global finance, trade, and currency regulation. That politics is hopeless, a farce, the attempt of financial and economic elites to come to some temporary arrangements

11   David Harvey, *The Enigma of Capital and the Crises of Capitalism*, New York: Oxford University Press, 2010, 216.

conducive to their continued exploitation of the work of the rest of us.

I've focused thus far on the Right's relation to the communist threat, that is, on the assumptions underpinning anticommunist rhetoric and attacks on the people. What about the democratic Left? Whereas the Right treats communism as a present force, the Left is bent around the force of loss, that is, the contorted shape it has found itself in as it has forfeited or betrayed the communist ideal.

The contemporary Left claims not to exist. Whereas the Right sees left-wing threats everywhere, those on the Left eschew any use of the term "we," emphasizing issue politics, identity politics, and their own fragmentation into a multitude of singularities. Writing in the wake of the announcement of the "death of communism," and challenging the adequacy of that description of the collapse of the Soviet Party-State, Badiou notes, "There is no longer a 'we,' there hasn't been one for a long time. The 'we' entered into its twilight well before the 'death of communism.'"[12] Over

12   Alain Badiou, *Of an Obscure Disaster—On the End of State-Truth*, trans. Barbara P. Fulks, Netherlands: Jan van

thirty years of unbridled capitalism made egoism and individualism the order of the day such that collectivity was already viewed with suspicion. The demise of the USSR didn't kill the "we."

The absence of a common program or vision is generally lamented, even as this absence is disconnected from the setting in which it appears as an absence, namely, the loss of a Left that says "we" and "our" and "us" in the first place. There are issues, events, projects, demonstrations, and affinity groups, but the Left claims not to exist. Left melancholics lament the lack of political alternatives when the real political alternative is the one whose loss determines their aimlessness—communism.[13]

Some on the Left view the lack of a common political vision or program as a strength.[14] They applaud what they construe as the freedom from the dictates of a party line and the opportunity to make individual choices

Eyck Academie and Arkzin d.o.o., 2009, 11.

13 As I detail in chapter five, the diagnosis of "left melancholia" comes from Wendy Brown, "Resisting Left Melancholia," *boundary 2* 26:3, 1999, 19–27.

14 For the definitive discussion of the theoretical tendencies characteristic of this "speculative left," see Bruno Bosteels, *The Actuality of Communism*, London: Verso, 2011.

with potentially radical political effects. The 2011 occupations of public squares in Spain and Greece are prime examples.[15] Opposing high unemployment and the imposition of austerity measures, hundreds of thousands took to the streets in a massive mobilization. Multiple voices—participants as well as commentators —emphasized that no common line, platform, or orientation united the protesters; they were not political. For many, the intense, festive atmosphere and break from the constraints of the usual politics incited a new confidence in social change. At the same time, the refusal of representation and reluctance to implement decision mechanisms hampered actual debate, enabling charismatic individual speakers to move the crowd and acquire quasi-leadership positions (no matter what position they took), and constraining the possibilities of working through political divergences toward a collective plan.

These same patterns reappeared in Occupy Wall Street. On the one hand, the openness of the movement, its rejection of party identification, made it initially inviting to a wide array of those who were discontented

15   C.G., "Democracy is born in the Squares," June 6, 2011, occupiedlondon.org.

with the continued unemployment, increasing inequality, and political stagnation in the US. On the other, when combined with the consensus-based process characteristic of the General Assemblies (adopted from the Spanish and Greek occupations), this inclusivity had detrimental effects, hindering the movement's ability to take a strong stand against capitalism and for collective control over common resources.

The disavowal of communism as a political ideal shapes the Left. Fragmented tributaries and currents, branches and networks of particular projects and partial objects, are the left form of the loss of communism. The "politics-of-no-politics" line seeking to trump class and economic struggle in the Spanish, Greek, and US protests wasn't new. For over thirty years, many on the Left have argued that this partial, dispersed politics is an advance over previous emphases on class and militancy (indeed, this is perhaps the strongest legacy of 1968). Avoiding the division and antagonism that comes with taking a political position, they displace their energies onto procedural concerns with inclusion and participation, as if the content of the politics were either given—a matter of identity—or secondary to the fact of inclusion, which makes the outcome of political struggle less significant than the process of struggle. These leftists name their goal democracy. They envision struggles on the Left specifically as struggles for democracy, rather than as struggles for the abolition of capitalism, collective ownership of the means of production, and economic equality within an already democratic setting.

An emphasis on democracy is radical in some settings, like in the French Revolution, the Haitian Revolution, the initial fight for political freedom that led to the Russian February Revolution, as well as in struggles against colonialism and imperialism, and even in opposition to the authoritarianism of the party-state bureaucracies of the former East. To stand for democracy was to stand against an order constituted through the exclusion of democracy. In contemporary parliamentary democracies, however, for leftists to refer to their goals as a struggle for democracy is strange. It is a defense of the status quo, a call for more of the same. Democracy is our ambient milieu, the hegemonic form of contemporary politics (which is yet another reason that the Right can use communism as a name for what opposes it). Left use of the language of democracy *now* avoids the fundamental antagonism between the 1 percent and the rest of us by acting as if the only thing really missing was participation.

Rather than recognizing that for the Left democracy is the form that the loss of communism takes, the form of communism's displacement, radical democrats treat democracy as itself replacing communism. The repercussion of the sublimation of communism in democratic preoccupations with process and participation is acquiescence to capitalism as the best system for the production and distribution of resources, labor, and goods.

Although the contemporary Left might seem to agree with the mainstream story of communism's failure—*it doesn't work*, where "it" holds the place for a wide variety of unspecified political endeavors—the language of failure covers over a more dangerous, anxiety-provoking idea—*communism succeeded*. The Left isn't afraid of failure. It is afraid of success, the successful mobilization of the energy and rage of the people. Leftists really fear the bloody violence of revolution, and hence they focus on displacing anger into safer procedural, consumerist, and aesthetic channels. As Peter Hallward emphasizes, the legacy of anti-Jacobinism is a preference for the condemnation of some kinds of violence but not others: leftists join democrats, liberals, and conservatives in denouncing the revolutionary Terror while they virtually ignore the "far more bloody repression of the 1871 Commune."[16] Even those who see themselves as part of some open and varied constellation of the Left condemn the violence of the people against those who would oppress them. State violence and the force of counterrevolution is taken for granted, assumed, cloaked in a prior legitimacy or presumed to be justified in the interest of order. Hallward writes, "From the perspective of what is already established, notes Saint-Just, 'that which produces the general good is always terrible.' The Jacobin terror was more defensive than aggressive, more a matter of restraining than of unleashing popular violence. 'Let us be terrible,' Danton said, 'so that the people need not be.'"[17] What is voiced on the Left as opposition to top-down organizing, vanguards, and elites, then, may well be the form taken by opposition to the unleashed fury of the people.

16 Peter Hallward, "Communism of the Intellect, Communism of the Will," in *The Idea of Communism*, ed. Costas Douzinas and Slavoj Žižek, London: Verso, 2010, 128.
17 Ibid.

Why would leftists fear a party in which we participate, rather than, say, understanding our participation
as influencing the shape, program, and actions of such
a party? Do we fear our own capacity for violence? Or
do we fear the uncontrollable force of the people mobilized against the system that exploits them, a force that
university gates are incapable of blocking? Perhaps
by recognizing this fear, leftists can concentrate it into
strength, that is, toward a confidence in the collective
power of the people to wipe out and remake.

The relation to collective power is the fundamental
difference between Right and Left. The Right emphasizes the individual, individual survival, individual
capacity, individual rights. The Left should be committed to the collective power of the people. As long as it
restricts itself to the conceptual vocabulary of individualism and democracy inhabited by the Right, as long
as it disperses collective energy into fleeting aesthetic
experiences and procedural accomplishments, the Left
will continue to lose the battle for equality.

The mistake leftists make when we turn into liberals and democrats is thinking that we are beyond the
communist horizon, that democracy replaced communism when it serves as the contemporary form

of communism's displacement. We don't see, can't
acknowledge, our own complicity in class struggle, in
capital's advances over the rest of us as working people.
It's as if we've forgotten that political struggle is an
irreducible dimension of capitalism—capital doesn't
cease pursuit of its own interests out of the goodness
of its cold and nonexistent heart. Capitalism always
and necessarily interlinks with conflict, resistance,
accommodation, and demands. Refusal to engage in
these struggles, rejection of the terms of these struggles, affects the form that capitalism takes. Absent the
discipline of unionized workers and an organized Left,
capital—particularly its strongest and most vicious
corporate and finance sectors—subsumes, appropri-
ates, and exploits everything it can.

Consider Luc Boltanski and Eve Chiapello's analysis of changes in management language from the sixties
to the nineties.[18] They document the dismantling of a
class-based approach to work and the assembling of
a new vision of work in terms of individual creativity,
autonomy, and flexibility. Personal benefits came to
outweigh collective action, thereby strengthening the

18   Luc Boltanski and Eve Chiapello, *The New Spirit of
Capitalism*, trans. Gregory Elliott, London: Verso, 2007.

position of employers. The resulting shift of responsibilities from organizations onto individuals undermined previous guarantees of security. The actuality of flexible employment was precarity—temporary work, subcontracting, project-based employment, multi-tasking, and opportunities contingent on personal networks. What matters here is the change in the understanding of work, a change from an emphasis on its class, group, and collective dimension to a view of work as a personal choice, endeavor, and locus of meaning. An idea of individual work displaced the sense of work as a common condition, thereby contributing to the liberation of capital from the constraints it encountered when it had to deal with workers as a collective force.

Evidence from the US confirms the shift from a class-based to an individualist conception of work as well as the negative impact of this shift on the economic well-being of the majority of the people. Historian Jefferson Cowie describes the individualist approach to work as it appears at the conjuncture of conflicting forces in the seventies. At the beginning of the decade, industrial workers rebelled against their containment within the post-war labor-liberal consensus. Relatively quickly, however, labor unrest blurred into the background of a wider variety of cultural conflicts around abortion, pornography, busing, crime, affirmative action, and gay rights. Cowie explains, "With class dissolving into ethnicity and resentment, inequality began to be perceived as a personal fate rather than a collective responsibility."[19] Accompanying the "internalization" of class struggle was an aggressive anti-union strategy on the part of corporations. This included a dramatic increase in pro-business lobbying, the legislative defeat of a major labor law reform bill, the migration of manufacturing from the North to the South (and off-shore), and an upsurge in direct and aggressive unfair labor practices, that is, acts that impeded workers' capacity to exercise their right to organize. By the end of the decade, workers were voting out unions. Finally, as the aggressive efforts of business organized as a class weakened labor as a collective force, the legal recognition of sex- and race-based discrimination itself had individualizing effects. Protections from discrimination and sexual harassment were secured through *individual* claims to violation and injury. The

19 Jefferson Cowie, *Stayin' Alive: The 1970s and the Last Days of the Working Class*, New York: The New Press, 2010, 216–217.

struggle for workplace equality thus involved a shift away from broad economic justice and "to a more individualistic terrain of 'occupational justice'—equal employment opportunity, diversity, affirmative action, and anti-harassment."[20] Workers had individual rights to be free from discrimination even as they were collectively becoming ever more exposed and vulnerable to a brutal capitalist economy.

A widely publicized study from Bruce Western and Jake Rosenfeld demonstrates that deunionization directly accounts for at least a third of the increase in income inequality experienced by US men working in the private sector. The indirect effects of the decline of unions are even more pronounced. Unions benefitted workers across the labor market insofar as they established a "moral economy," a set of expectations of equity, solidarity, and fairness with broad social, cultural, and political resonance. Western and Rosenfeld write, "The decline of American labor and the associated increase in wage inequality signaled the deterioration of the labor market as a political institution. Workers became less connected to each other in

20   Ibid., 239.

their organizational lives and less connected in their economic fortunes."[21] When work was understood in terms of class, collective expectations provided a potent counterforce to capital. The shift to an individualist conception of work undermined that force.

For the Left, democracy is the form the loss of communism takes. Rather than fighting for a collective ideal, engaging in a struggle on behalf of the rest of us, the Left repetitively invokes democracy, calling for what is already there. These invocations of democracy take on a pattern that Lacan describes via the psychoanalytic notion of drive. Like desire, drive refers to a way that the subject arranges her enjoyment (*jouissance*). With respect to desire, enjoyment is what the subject can never reach, what the subject wants but never gets—*oh, that's not it*. Drive differs in that enjoyment comes from missing one's goal; it's what the subject gets, even if she doesn't want it.[22] Enjoyment is that little extra

21 Bruce Western and Jake Rosenfeld, "Unions, Norms, and the Rise in American Wage Inequality," *American Sociological Review* 76: 4, 2011, 513–537.
22 See Slavoj Žižek, *The Ticklish Subject*, London: Verso, 2000.

charge which keeps the subject keeping on. The subject's repeated yet ever failing efforts to reach her goal become satisfying on their own.

Left appeals to democracy take on the structure of the drive insofar as they circle around and around. We perpetually miss our goal and get satisfaction through this very missing. Or we don't even have an actual goal, and we take the absence of a goal to be a strength. We talk, complain, and protest. We make groups on Facebook. We sign petitions and forward them to everyone in our contact list. Activity becomes passivity, our stuckness in a circuit, which is then mourned as the absence of ideas or even the loss of the political itself and then routed yet again through a plea for democracy, although it doesn't take a genius to know that the real problem is capitalism. What leftists call the loss of the political is the fog they wander through because they've lost sight of the communist horizon.

Some contemporary theorists commend drive's sublimation, its substitution of partial objects and the bits of enjoyment accompanying repetitions of a process for the impossible object of desire. Multiple voices in networked and digital media circuits, for example, celebrate communicative capitalism for its provision of opportunities for small victories and momentary pleasures. Millions die in war and poverty, but at least we have the internet. Others admire drive's creative destruction, the way its dissolution of the old is the opening to the new. Admittedly, repeating the same act over and over can shift from order to chaos—it's one thing to scratch an itch a couple of times; it's something else entirely to claw through to the bone. The reiterations that fail to respond to changes in their setting themselves change the setting. But the embrace of drive as destruction, like the view of drive as sublimation, treats a feature of our setting as an alternative without drawing the necessary separation: what makes it a feature of a different formation, a different politics, or even a critique?

In the contemporary networks of communicative capitalism, drive is a feedback circuit that captures our best energies. Invigorating communism as a political alternative requires amplifying the collective desire that can cut through these affective networks.

Chapter Three

Sovereignty of the People

I've discussed communism as a tag for two features of our current setting, the past Soviet experiment and a present force. I've described the present force of communism via a right-left distinction between threat and loss, a distinction which rests on a common supposition of democracy. The Right positions communism as a continued threat to democracy. The Left is stuck in democratic drive as the actuality of its suppression of communist desire. In each instance, communism names that in opposition to which our current setting is configured, the setting within which contemporary capitalism unfolds.

Why is communism that name? Because it designates the sovereignty of the people, and not the people as a whole or a unity but the people as the *rest of us*, those of us whose work, lives, and futures are expropriated, monetized, and speculated on for the financial enjoyment of the few. Georg Lukács invokes the people in just this sense when he explains the dialectical transformation of the concept of the people in Lenin's characterization of the Russian Revolution: "The vague and abstract concept of 'the people' had to be rejected, but only so that a revolutionary, discriminating, concept of 'the people'—*the revolutionary alliance of the oppressed*—could develop from a concrete understanding of the conditions of proletarian revolution."[1] In this chapter, I present the idea of the people as the rest of us as a modulation of the idea of the proletariat as the subject of communism.

When the people are the subject of communism, their sovereignty is not that of the dispersed individuals of liberal democracy. Rather, the sovereignty of the people corresponds to the political form Marxist theory refers to as the dictatorship of the proletariat, the direct and fearsome rule of the collective people over those who would oppress and exploit them, over those who would take for themselves what belongs to all in common.[2] As

1   Georg Lukács, *Lenin: A Study on the Unity of His Thought*, trans. Nicholas Jacobs, London: Verso, 2009, 22–23.
2   For an account of the idea of dictatorship and its association with popular sovereignty in the setting in which Marx and Engels were writing, see Hal Draper, *The Dictatorship of the*

Lenin describes it in *State and Revolution*, the dictatorship of the proletariat is an organization of the oppressed for the purpose of suppressing the oppressor. More than a mere expansion of democracy, more than the inclusion of more people within democracy's purview, the dictatorship of the proletariat puts into practice the purpose and end of democracy, making it serve the many and not the "money-bags." Consequently and necessarily, the dictatorship of the proletariat imposes restrictions: it restricts the freedom of capitalists, exploiters, and oppressors. They are not free to do as they will but are governed, controlled, and limited by the rest of us. In time, this governance, control, and limitation effectively eliminate the capitalist class. But until the inequality that enables capitalism has been eliminated, the organized power of a state serves as the instrument through which the people not only govern, but insure that governance is carried out for the benefit of the collective rather than the few.

Proletariat from Marx to Lenin, New York: Monthly Review Press, 1987, esp. ch. 1. For a contemporary defense of the idea of the dictatorship of the proletariat, see Étienne Balibar, *On the Dictatorship of the Proletariat*, trans. Grahame Locke, London: Verso, 1977.

An advantage of the Marxist view of the proletariat as the subject of communism is its linkage of an essential role in production to an essential role in politics. The proletariat has been a name for the universal class, the subject-object of history, because its emancipation emancipates us all, dissolving the class and property relations at the basis of capitalist power. The proletarian is not just the worker; the proletarian is the worker radicalized, the worker politicized. Lenin, for example, embraced the "merger narrative," the idea (originally elaborated by Karl Kautsky) that Marx's unique achievement was merging two previously separate political elements—working class struggle and socialism—into a single narrative that makes establishing socialism into the *goal* of the workers' struggle, in fact, into the *historical mission* of the working class.[3]

The merger narrative has organizational and political repercussions. It establishes the responsibility of the socialist party to bring to the workers the "good news" of their political position. The task of socialists is "to organize the proletariat politically, to fill it with

3   See Lars T. Lih, *Lenin Rediscovered*, Chicago, IL: Haymarket Books, 2008.

the awareness of its position and its task, and to make and keep it spiritually and physically fit for struggle."[4] The merger narrative generally, as well as Lenin's specific extension of it into the Russian context, presupposes the active militancy of workers' struggles, an assumption that fit empirically with the rising oppositional force of factory workers in the nineteenth century. A spirit of resistance is already present in the workers, pushing them toward organized struggle. The party channels and orients these active workers' struggles toward socialism. It provides political direction to an already active force.

Does this narrative make sense for us? Does it make sense for leftists living in the US, UK, and EU to continue to think in terms of the leading role of the proletariat? That the words "proletariat" and "bourgeoisie" feel strange in our mouths likely indicates the depth of capitalist ideology, the extent of the class power of an elite that has gotten us to think in terms of competition, efficiency, stock markets, bonuses, and financial success. Truly obscene is the spread of the term "branding" such that one can speak of

4   Ibid., 48.

"rebranding" Marxism, feminism, and the Left without irony. The power of organized capital may well account for why few in the US think in terms of "proletariat" and "bourgeoisie." But it does not prevent us from recognizing class, work, division, inequality, and privilege (although it certainly tries), all of which are visible, tangible, unavoidable. My wager, then, is that an emphasis on the people as the rest of us can do the work formerly done by "proletariat."

Another reason to endorse the idea of the people as the rest of us involves the limitations of the figuration of the proletariat as the industrial working class. To be sure, Marx and Marxists don't reduce "proletariat" to an empirical designator of one specific type of worker. In his note to the 1888 English edition of the "Communist Manifesto," Engels says that "proletariat" refers to "the class of modern wage-laborers who, having no means of production of their own, are reduced to selling their labor-power in order to live." In a similar vein, Étienne Balibar writes, "The proletariat is not a homogeneous unchanging group, which bears its name and its fate clearly inscribed once and for all, for all to see. It is the historical result of the permanent process by which it is constituted, which is the other side of the process of accumulation of capital."[5] Engels and Balibar make clear that the proletariat is not a pure or fixed class. Rather than a static social group, *proletarianization* is a dynamic, the process through which capitalism produces, uses up, and discards the workers it needs (a process facilitated by capitalist use of the state). This process impacts the majority of people in the US, UK, and EU, not to mention China, Brazil, and other countries experiencing rapid and dramatic urbanization as peasants leave the land and move to cities looking for work. Embracing the idea of the people as the rest of us acknowledges that the merger narrative responded to a specific composition of social, political, and technological forces. This composition has changed even as proletarianization as a broad process with a range of effects persists.[6]

In the US, the political power of organized labor has diminished together with the substantial decline in private sector union membership, the spread of an individualist conception of work, and the realignments within the Democratic Party. The importance

5 Balibar, *On the Dictatorship of the Proletariat*, 83–84.
6 Michael Hardt, "The Common in Communism," *Rethinking Marxism* 22:3, 2010, 346–356.

of manufacturing and industrial production has likewise decreased as the US economy has shifted away
from the production of goods and toward the provision
of services. According to historian Judith Stein, the
US "traded factories for finance," a process generally linked to a shift to neoliberal economic policies.[7]
Doug Henwood notes that in 1991, "finance, insurance, and real estate, collectively nicknamed 'FIRE,'
surpassed manufacturing's contribution to GDP, and
widened their lead in subsequent years."[8] As of May
2010, the occupations with the highest percentage of
US employees were retail salespersons, cashiers, office
clerks, food preparation and food service workers,
nurses, waiters and waitresses, and customer service
representatives.[9] In 1969, one-third of jobs in the US
were in goods-producing industries; in 2007, only 16
percent of jobs were.[10] If proletarianization initially

7   Judith Stein, *Pivotal Decade*, New Haven, CT: Yale
University Press, 2010, xii.

8   Doug Henwood, *Wall Street*, London: Verso, 1998, 76.

9   Bureau of Labor Statistics, "Retail salespersons: occupation with highest employment in 2010," May 20, 2011, US
Department of Labor, bls.gov.

10   Lawrence Mishel, Jared Bernstein, and Heidi Shierholz,
The State of Working America, Ithaca, NY: ILR and Cornell

designated the process by which those with land were disappropriated of it, contemporary proletarianization is the expropriation of secure, decently waged, skilled jobs and the creation of servants (who are required to smile, care, communicate, and be friendly).

The shift from manufacturing to service is not unique to the US. Between 1970 and 2010, Germany, Italy, France, Japan, Sweden, the Netherlands, Canada, Australia, the US, and the UK experienced declines in the percentage of people employed in manufacturing and increases in the percentage of people employed in services. The drop in the UK was highest at 23.9 percent.[11] The changes in capitalism these statistics mark, changes usually discussed under the headings of deindustrialization, post-Fordism, and the rise of a knowledge- or information-based economy, suggest the inapplicability of the figure of the industrial proletariat as the contemporary subject of communism (a point that already has a legacy in communist movements that relied on a mobilized peasantry). Yes, there is still

University Press, 2009, 232.
11   Bureau of Labor Statistics, "Charting Annual Comparisons of International Labor Force Statistics, 2010," US Department of Labor, bls.gov.

industry and there is still manufacturing. But changes in both associated with the diffusion and application of information and communication technologies, as well as with the political assault on working people ideologically organized as neoliberalism, suggest the limits of an opposition imagined as organized primarily in terms of factory labor.

Michael Hardt and Antonio Negri view the changes brought about by deindustrialization, the rise of service sector work, and the expansion of technologies as indicative of the need for a concept more flexible and inclusive than "proletariat." They offer "multitude" as an alternative. The multitude is a generative and creative force, the productive power that capitalism depends on, mobilizes, and tries to control. Yet the concept includes too much—everyone in fact— and the cost of this inclusion is antagonism. Rather than labor against capital, haves against have-nots, the 99 percent against the 1 percent, we have a multitude of singularities combining and recombining in mobile, fluid, communicative, and affective networks. "Multitude" fits better with production under communicative capitalism than "proletarian," particularly insofar as Hardt and Negri emphasize the crucial role of global information and communication networks. Under communicative capitalism, the idea of a subject-object of history resonates less with a sociological class than with feedback loops, organized networks, and emergent formations wherein we bring ourselves into being as something new, where we are the objects of our activity, making our own setting and configuring our world. But the problem of multitude's inability to express division remains.

Jacques Rancière's notion of the "part-of-no-part" helps solve the problems of the inclusive multitude. He develops the concept in the context of a reading of Plato and Aristotle, a reading where he shows the operation of a miscount in the counting of the parties to politics. Although the ancients treat the people as a part of the *polis*, as a group with properties comparable to the wealth of the oligarchs and the virtue of aristocrats, the people actually have nothing. Their vaunted freedom is more properly understood as a fiction standing in for the absence of wealth and virtue. It is a fiction to say that freedom is exclusively a property of the people since freedom is what the people have in common with the rich and noble. This fiction exerts a powerful force: treating as specific what is in fact common, it allows the *demos* "to identify with the whole of the community through homonymy." The freedom that is common to all, the people claim as their own. Even as they have no part of anything, no wealth and no virtue, this part-of-no-part identifies itself as the community. Rancière writes, "Whoever has no part—the poor of ancient times, the third estate, the modern proletariat—cannot in fact have any part other than all or nothing."[12] The part-of-no-part thus does not designate the objectivity of an empirical group excluded from the political domain. It's not another way of referring to a politics of identity by locating a marginalized other. Nor is it a synonym for the proletariat. Rather, the part-of-no-part designates the *interruption* of a given order by those who have no part.

Rancière's concept of the part-of-no-part provides a way to think about the people as the rest of us, of the people as a dividing and divisive force. When the people are conceived as the part of those who have no part, we are prevented from reducing the people to an empirical given or treating the people as the totality of the community. Instead, the people mark and are

12 Jacques Rancière, *Disagreement*, trans. Julie Rose, Minneapolis, MN: University of Minnesota Press, 2004, 9.

marked by a gap. They are qualified, politicized by the crime and injustice that has deprived them of a part (of wealth and of virtue in the ancient texts).

The part-that-is-not-a-part designates a gap in an existing order between that order and other possible arrangements. The Lacanian synonym for the part-of-no-part is *objet petit a*, an impossible, formal object produced as the excess of a process or relation, a kind of gap that incites or annoys, the missingness or not-quite-rightness that calls out to us, Santner's signifying stress. Introducing a Lacanian synonym accentuates the fact that this part is not a substantial part, not an empirical designator such that exclusion is the exclusion of people and their inclusion necessarily a political good. For example, "religious fundamentalist" might be a name for the part with no part in a liberal order. To include that part would distort and disrupt the order predicated on the exclusion of fundamentalist religion. "Capitalist" names one with no part in a communist order. To include the capitalist would undermine an order based on the abolition of private property and exploitation. In sum, the benefit of Rancière's part-of-no-part is not that it takes the place of the universal class or names a new historical subject-object. It's that it indicates an inflection and qualification of the people, its non-coincidence with itself.

While the people as the rest of us, as the part-of-no-part, is better than "proletariat" and "multitude" as a designator for the contemporary subject of communism, class struggle remains essential as the name for the fundamental antagonism through which society emerges—the division between the rich and the rest of us. "Class struggle" marks the fact that there is no set of ordered relations constitutive of sociality as such.[13] There is no society in which every element fully occupies a place. Instead, society arises through failures and solutions, combinations, repressions, divisions, and exclusions. Society is incomplete, ruptured, and contested. "Class struggle" designates this incompleteness, rupture, and contestation rather than the positivity of a conflict between empirically given and demographically conceived social groups. Capitalism, as Marx makes clear in his famous account of primitive accumulation, is an *effect* of class struggle

We can also say that capitalism is another term for class struggle as it manifests itself in a given mode

13   For further discussion see my *Žižek's Politics*, New York: Routledge, 2006, 55–60.

of production. Žižek writes, "class struggle cannot be reduced to a conflict between particular agents within social reality; it is not a difference between agents (which can be described by means of a detailed social analysis), but an antagonism ('struggle') which constitutes these agents."[14] Classes don't preexist the struggles that produce them, struggles fought on multiple terrains—cultural, legal, technological, national and other such instantiations of past struggles. And because classes don't preexist these struggles, their politics is not given in advance as a necessary outgrowth of inevitable or naturalistically conceived interests. The opposition that "class struggle" designates is open to political determination. It can be configured in religious, nationalist, populist, libertarian, and other directions. The challenge for communists is thus not to identify a particular class vanguard but to clarify why communism is the best alternative to capitalism and to participate in organizing and furthering the struggle toward it.

Žižek's reading of Lacan provides a further argument against the relevance for us of the merger narrative

14 Slavoj Žižek, *Living in the End Times*, London: Verso 2011, 201.

and its ordination of the proletariat into its historical mission: the big Other doesn't exist. There is no big Other of History, no story of inevitable progress or the realization of freedom in the world that can ground or guarantee our actions. Contingency and the multiplicity of determinations accompany systems, patterns, and path dependencies. Human actions, whether planned or unplanned, organized or individual—as well as unpredictable events and the complex, interconnected, and unforeseen effects of human and non-human actions—impact the processes and flows retroactively understood as history. Rather than given by the logic of history, political choices are unavoidably open and uncertain. Something can always go horribly wrong. With respect to the merger narrative, leftists have had to grapple with the fact that history hasn't unfolded according to socialist predictions. Socialism did not lead to communism. The workers of the world did not unite. Capitalism has been relatively successful in adapting in response to the crises it generates, in large part through the ruling classes' use of state power. We no longer have recourse to the historical narrative that made building communism the mission of the proletariat.

The unraveling of the merger narrative does not mean that workers do not struggle against capitalist exploitation. Nor does it mean that workers do not rise up against states that govern on behalf of a ruling capitalist class. It means that there is nothing given or inevitable about the political shape of unavoidable class struggle, a struggle that Marx and Engels understood in the broad terms of the antagonism between those who are forced to sell their labor power to survive and those who are not. While they described this as a struggle between the bourgeoisie as owners of the means of production and the proletariat as wage-laborers, in the contemporary US, UK, and EU, this opposition makes more sense as one between the rich and the rest of us.

A substantial portion of the super-rich does not own the means of production; they are CEOs of corporations that are publicly held. They are employees, although their astronomical annual salaries and bonuses exceed what most of the rest of us will be paid in a lifetime. After a year or so of that, bankers and hedge fund managers cannot be said to be "forced to sell their labor power to survive." As with the capitalism of the Gilded Age, neoliberal capitalism relies on the hegemony of finance, the concentration of power in financial institutions. Duménil and Lévy explain that "neoliberalism is a social order aimed at the generation of income for the upper income brackets, not investment in production nor, even less, social progress. In countries of the center, domestic capital accumulation was sacrificed in favor of income distribution benefitting the upper classes."[15] Contemporary capitalism is less oriented toward producing things than it is toward financial and commercial practices that benefit the 1 percent, supporting their continued and increasing consumption. Some of the rest of us are employed in the service of this financial and corporate elite, perhaps as accountants and consultants, maybe as culture, food, health, and transportation providers, a few as trainers of their young. An even larger percentage of the rest of us are unemployed, underemployed, retired, disabled, and unremunerated for much of the work that we do (particularly caregiving work). Worldwide, at least a billion of us find ourselves doing work for free that corporations claim to own. Perhaps the best known example

15 Gérard Duménil and Dominique Lévy, *The Crisis of Neoliberalism*, Cambridge, MA: Harvard University Press, 2011, 22.

of this capitalization of unpaid labor is Facebook, the CEO of which is the youngest billionaire in the world. Nearly every time we go online or use a mobile phone we produce for someone else, creating the data and traces that this someone else claims to own. Our collective actions create the rich. They can also destroy them.

The "people as the rest of us" designates those of us who are proletarianized by capitalism, the people produced through the exploitation, extraction, and expropriation of our practical and communicative activities for the enjoyment of the very, very rich. When communism is our horizon of political possibility, the sovereignty of the people points to a view of the state as what *we* use to govern for *us* as a collectivity. It is our collective steering of our common future for our common good.

Michel Foucault's insight into the limitation of sovereign knowledge crucial to economic liberalism provides an opening for theorizing communism as the sovereignty of the people. In his 1978–1979 lectures published as *The Birth of Biopolitics*, Foucault presents the shift from absolutism to liberalism in Europe (primarily England, France, and Germany) at the end of the eighteenth century as a change in governmental reason. Foucault argues that the change turns on the emergence of a new domain of truth, a domain that provides new criteria by which to assess governance as well as a new model of the subject. The emergence of this new domain of truth hollows out sovereign power, redirecting the authority and reason previously assembled in the state into a civil society that itself comes into being through this redirection.

The new domain was political economy. Political economy provides the material for assessing government as it discovers a set of natural processes with their own laws of supply and demand, logics of causes and effects, and determinations of incentives and consequences. For political economy, these processes, particularly as they seem to obey spontaneous mechanisms, are a site of truth, the truth of the natural limitations of government. The sovereign *may have a right* to levy taxes, but is that *good government*? Foucault explains that to ask this question is to install a limitation on sovereign power, fundamentally changing the logic of governance. If truth is located in the market, it is displaced from juridically determined principles of right, the principles championed by natural law theorists as well as by the French Revolution. The reason for and measure of governance is thus absent from the state. Once truth is invested in the market, once the market emerges as a site of veridiction, the task of government becomes securing, circumscribing, and supervising this site.[16]

Homo economicus, economic man, is the subject appropriate to the new field of political economy. Bound up in a world he can neither predict nor control, economic man's interests depend on a series of accidents, on actions and others which he cannot and does not know. Economic man's situation, Foucault explains, is "therefore doubly involuntary, indefinite, and non-totalizable."[17] Yet—and here is the mystery of the invisible hand—in these conditions of collective blindness, each is said to be able to benefit. In fact, these conditions of collective blindness are posited as *necessary* conditions for each to benefit. Any attempt to ensure something like the public good must fail because collective benefit can *only* be secured through the pursuit of individual self-interest.

16   Michel Foucault, *The Birth of Biopolitics*, trans. Graham Burchell, New York: Palgrave Macmillan, 2008, 116.
17   Ibid., 278.

Just as individual economic actors cannot see the whole, neither can the sovereign: a visible hand would be no hand at all. It would be partial, distorted. It would fail to combine the multitude of economic interests. Political economy proclaims that "there is no sovereign in economics. There is no economic sovereign." As Foucault writes, *homo economicus* "tells the sovereign: You must not. But why must he not? You must not because you cannot. And you cannot in the sense that 'you are powerless.' And why are you powerless, why can't you? You cannot because you do not know, and you not know because you cannot know." Economic man thus does not simply limit sovereign power. Rather, he "strips the sovereign of power inasmuch as he reveals an essential, fundamental, and major incapacity of the sovereign, that is to say, an inability to master the totality of the economic field."[18] Liberalism's embrace of political economy hollows out juridical sovereignty by positing an ensemble of mutually conditioning choices and decisions, knowledge of which necessarily eludes the sovereign.

The hollowing out of sovereign power allows for

18   Ibid., 283, 292.

various resolutions. One would be a kind of zoning of sovereignty that excludes the sovereign from the market. Another would hold the sovereign responsible for supervising and verifying market processes. In this second version, the very practices of governmental activities associated with supervision would subordinate sovereign reason to "a scientific and speculative rationality."[19] What actually happens, Foucault explains, is a third course, one that extends government into a new domain—civil society. As a new field for the exercise of governmental power, civil society provides a location for the management of economic men. It's a plane of reference where individuals are governed not as subjects of right or as economic actors but through a new ensemble that merges juridical and market concerns as it brings other elements (health, education, reproduction) into relation with them.

The sovereignty that liberalism (and, later, neoliberalism) hollows out is the sovereignty of the people —not the people as individuals, who are included as agents in civil society who buy, sell, and contract, but the people as a *collective* body with the capacity

19   Ibid., 292.

for domination. Benjamin Constant's liberal embrace of private wealth over Rousseau's general will, for example, relies on the idea that individualizing economic forces are ultimately more powerful than collectivizing political ones. Constant writes:

> Money is the most effective curb on despotism...
> Force is useless against it: money conceals itself or flees ... Among the ancients, credit did not have the importance it has for us today. Their governments were more powerful than private individuals. Today, by contrast, private individuals are everywhere stronger than political power. Wealth is a force that is more readily exerted on all interests, and consequently it is far more real and *more readily obeyed*.[20]

Constant merges the power of money with the power of the individual. Avoiding the fact that only very, very rich individuals have enough money to be stronger than governments, his story of curbing despotism is also one of the rise of a real and powerful force exerting itself on the people.

20   Quoted in Luciano Canfora, *Democracy in Europe*, trans. Simon Jones, Malden, MA: Blackwell Publishing, 2006, 64.

In Foucault's exposition, the theoretical problem that emerges at the end of the eighteenth and the beginning of the nineteenth century is the incompatibility between governance conceived via the subject of right and will and governance conceived via the subject of interest. Whereas the former requires a splitting and renunciation, traditionally expressed as a social contract through which individuals come together as a unity by agreeing to a set of self-imposed constraints, the latter requires, even enjoins, the subject to pursue his self-interest. As political economy, moreover, this latter liberal conception establishes a field and frame for this pursuit of self-interest, a field and frame that becomes the site of freedom as well as a new domain of truth. Foucault writes, "Liberalism acquired its modern shape precisely with the formulation of this essential incompatibility between the non-totalizable multiplicity of economic subjects of interest and the totalizing unity of the juridical sovereign."[21] A certain version of the economy, one first focused on the market and then on a narrow, odd notion of competition, is presented as a barrier to governance, as a limit on what

21   Foucault, *The Birth of Biopolitics*, 282.

government can know and do. The emergence of this limit accompanies the spread of democracy in Europe, understood both in terms of ideas of natural right, the social contract, and the juridical will and in terms of the instantiation of these ideas via extensions of suffrage and the institutionalization of mass parties.

Liberal political economy is a limiting of the people as a collective force with the will to oversee, guide, direct, and organize economic matters. It's an incapacitating of collective strength, a fragmenting of it into suppositions of individuals already competing and opposed (a point Marx explains in "On the Jewish Question"). As Foucault makes clear in his discussion of civil society, the limiting of the collective power of the people turns them from active agents into a passive population. They are active only as individuals, little entrepreneurs or enterprises. What appears as the freedom of the market thus depends on the foreclosure of the collective power of the people over what they share and produce in common. The power that matters—that of the people to affect the basic conditions in which they live—a power only actual if it is collective, is displaced onto an economy that they are told they cannot govern because they cannot know. The economy acts because the people cannot. As they are limited to their individual singularity, the economy gains the force and power of collective energies and engagements.

The liberal hollowing out of sovereignty depends on the claim that sovereignty requires total knowledge; sovereignty over the economy is ostensibly impossible because economic processes cannot be known. We don't need to accept this claim. Neither sovereign power nor sovereign knowledge is ever whole or complete. They are partial, changing, and mutually determining. They are open to revision, recombination, and contestation. The sovereignty of the people doesn't stem from what we know; it arises from what we do: we create the world that creates us.

If Foucault provides a negative approach to the sovereignty of the people as that collective force capable of guiding production and distribution according to a common will—that is, if his account of liberalism and neoliberalism enables this force to appear as what political economy forecloses—then Susan Buck-Morss offers a more direct route to the same point. She explains that Soviet legal theory rests the socialist state on the political sovereignty of the working people; the dictatorship of the proletariat is explicitly and literally the name for the sovereignty of the people.[22] Drawing from French historian François Furet, Buck-Morss positions the dictatorship of the proletariat in the political trajectory extending out of the French Revolution. The dictatorship of the proletariat realizes the power of the people by establishing an impossible identity between government and the governed. As Žižek puts it, *"'the dictatorship of the proletariat' is another name for the violence of the democratic explosion itself."*[23]

Buck-Morss criticizes this rendition of the sovereignty of the people for relying on a trick: the unity of the people does not preexist the violence and exclusion that calls it into being. Such violence, typically exercised via the naming and elimination of an enemy, cannot be justified. Those who would justify it are not yet constituted as a collective. The excess of power thus marks the point of nonidentity between the people and their sovereignty, that is to say, the gap between

22   Susan   Buck-Morss,   *Dreamworld   and   Catastrophe*, Cambridge, MA: MIT Press, 2002, 19.
23   Slavoj Žižek, *In Defense of Lost Causes*, London: Verso, 2008, 416.

government and the governed. Buck-Morss writes, "When democratic sovereignty *confronts* the people with all the violence that it monopolizes as the legitimate embodiment *of* the people, it is in fact attesting to its *non*identity with the people."[24] For Buck-Morss, the repercussion of this nonidentity is a vicious circle or "wild zone" where legality and illegality become indistinguishable. Where it would ostensibly guarantee legitimacy on the basis of wholeness, of the unity of the *demos*, the sovereignty of the people mobilizes division instead.

Žižek's account of "retroactive determination" solves the problem of the "wild zone." No decision is fully covered in advance of its being made. Not only can it always come into question, but the decision itself contributes to the setting in which it comes into question. (The political correlate is calling into being those who would justify the call.) Exposure, then, is not a problem specific to sovereignty. It's an aspect of the structure of law in all its complexity, indeterminacy, and command. At any given point, the legal status of a ruling may be uncertain, dependent on enforcement or

24   Buck-Morss, *Dreamworld and Catastrophe*, 7.

interpretation, waiting in the courts, subject to appeal, in the process of being contested, amended, and reinterpreted. A precedent is only a precedent after it is upheld as such—and then it can still be broken and disavowed. The instability between legal and illegal inheres to law. It is not specific to a democratic instantiation of sovereignty.

More important is Buck-Morss's emphasis on the nonidentity of the people with its sovereignty, on the missing link between the people and government. Although she treats the mobilization of this division as the problem, I see it as the crucial materialist component of the notion of the people as the subject of communism. Division separates the people of communism from the imagined totality of the people of populism. Rather than there being a smooth (naturalized) flow from actual people to the collective power of the sovereign people, a gap disrupts the whole, belying the fantasy of the whole thing or order. No matter how popular the sovereign, the people and the government are not present at the same time. Where the people are present, there is chaos, disruption. Where government is present, then the people are not. Insofar as the people can never be fully present—some don't show up, didn't hear what was going on, were mislead by a powerful speaker, were miscounted from the outset, completely disagreed and so wanted to count themselves out, were barred from attending—their necessary absence is the gap of politics. In Rancière's words, "the reality denoted by the terms 'worker,' 'people' or 'proletarian' could never be reduced either to the positivity of a material condition nor to the superficial conceit of an imaginary, but always designated a partial (in both senses) linkage, provisional and polemical, of fragments of experience and forms of symbolization."[25] Split, divided, impossible, the people cannot *be* politically. They are only political through and as one, few, or some (never as a direct embodiment, only as limit): one represents us to ourselves as many; few make possible and organize, provide themes and ideas; some do all the work. The people are always non-all, not simply because the many is open and incomplete but because it cannot totalize itself. The rule of a leader, party, or constitution compensates for or occupies the hole of the missing conjunction between people and

25   Jacques Rancière, *Staging the People: The Proletarian and His Double*, trans. David Fernbach, London: Verso, 2011, 14.

government. Nonetheless, this rule cannot overcome the division that the sovereignty of the people mobilizes; division goes all the way down—antagonism is fundamental, irreducible.

Giorgio Agamben also notes the nonidentity of the people. Rather than construing this nonidentity in terms of the gap of sovereignty, Agamben considers how the referent of the people shifts from all to some, from a mythic, impossible, *all of us* to the division between the privileged and the rest of us. He writes, "It is as if what we call 'people' were in reality not a unitary subject but a dialectical oscillation between two opposite poles: on the one hand, the set of the People as a whole political body, and, on the other, the subset of the people as a fragmentary multiplicity of needy and excluded bodies."[26] The constitutive division within the people expresses itself in language. The term can refer to an imagined unity of everyone, as it seems to do in the expression "the sovereignty of the people." It can also refer to the less well off, the poor, the workers, the exploited, the majority whose lives and labor are expropriated to benefit the few. To appeal to the people

26   Giorgio Agamben, *Homo Sacer*, trans. Daniel Heller-Roazen, Stanford, CA: Stanford University Press, 1998, 177.

in this second sense is to express and politicize a division between the few and the many, to make the many appear in their need and in their power.

Agamben's "dialectical oscillation" nonetheless stops too soon. It oscillates between two positions, although there is a third, where the needy, producing bodies *are* the political body (sovereign), and even a fourth, where *the fact* that the needy, producing bodies are the political body *makes the impossibility of totalizing or enclosing the political as a body appear*. Even without these additional moves, though, Agamben's language confounds the reading of the division in the people that I suggest. He splices together different images of division. That is, Agamben refers to two opposite poles and to a unified whole and what is excluded from it. A division between opposite poles is a division within a field (we could even say a field characterized by extension and without necessary boundaries). A division between a whole and what's outside it displaces this internal division, thereby rendering the open field into a unitary body. The political problem thereby shifts from an opposition within the people, between exploiters and the exploited, to one of being excluded from the people (the problem that preoccupies Buck-Morss). The corresponding political solution then appears as inclusion and the initial matter of division and opposition within the people is effaced.

A better way to conceive the division within the people, one capable of expressing the power of the people in and as a collectivity but not as a whole and not as a unity, makes use of the psychoanalytic distinction between desire and drive.[27] While Freud's vicissitudes of the drive are generally known (reversal into its opposite, turning round upon the subject's own self, repression, and sublimation), two features of the perhaps less familiar Lacanian notion of drive bear emphasizing. The first concerns the difference between drive and desire as relations of *jouissance*, in other words, as economies through which the subject structures her enjoyment. Desire is always a desire to desire, a desire that can never be filled, a desire for a *jouissance* or enjoyment that can never be attained.[28] In contrast, drive attains *jouissance* in the repetitive

27   See Jodi Dean, "Drive as the Structure of Biopolitics," *Krisis* 2, 2010.
28   Slavoj Žižek, *The Ticklish Subject*, London: Verso, 2000, 291.

process of not reaching it. One doesn't have to reach the goal to enjoy. Enjoyment attaches to the process, thereby capturing the subject. Enjoyment, no matter how small, fleeting, or partial, is why one persists in the loop of drive. The second feature concerns the different status of *objet petit a* in desire and drive. Žižek writes:

> Although, in both cases, the link between object and loss is crucial, in the case of the *objet a* as the object of *desire*, we have an object which was originally lost, which coincides with its own loss, which emerges as lost, while, in the case of the *objet a* as the object of drive, the "object" *is directly the loss itself*—in the shift from desire to drive, we pass from the *lost object* to *loss itself as an object*. That is to say, the weird movement called "drive" is not driven by the "impossible" quest for the lost object; it is *a push to directly enact the "loss"—the gap, cut, distance—itself.*[29]

Drive is a force that is shaped from loss. It is loss as a force, or the force loss exerts on the field of desire.

29   Žižek, *In Defense of Lost Causes*, 328.

The people as desiring have needs, needs they can only address together, collectively, active and in common. Their sovereignty can be reduced neither to their majority nor to their procedures. Rather, it names the cause and reason for government: the collective people in their desire for a common good. The people as caught in drive are fragmented, dispersed into networks and tributaries. Stuck in drive's repetitive loops, they pursue their separate enterprises even as they are governmentalized objects, a population.

I engage Buck-Morss and Agamben not only to get at a view of communism as the force of the people as sovereign in the economy. I also want to emphasize that for communists, the binary inclusion/exclusion does not indicate the primary axis of justice. The conceptual benefit of the notion of the sovereignty of the people is that it is *not* all inclusive; it is divisive. (For liberal democrats, however, who insist that the true political issue is making sure that no one is excluded from opportunities to participate in the democratic process or from the possibility of striking it rich in the capitalist market, the inclusion/exclusion binary functions quite nicely.) For example, a pressing contemporary issue concerns undocumented workers. The remedy to the problem of those without papers is to get them papers—and thus membership in the state. This isn't a bad goal, but it is a goal that extends rather than takes or changes state power. Similarly, some argue that the solution to the dilemma posed by increasing millions of slum dwellers is a right to property, a remedy that incorporates the owner into the official market economy, in effect eliminating the threat to the market that uncounted use and exchange pose. This is not a communist position because capitalism is a system that constitutively exploits people, not one that constitutively excludes them.

Building from Badiou and Rancière, Žižek claims that the antagonism between the included and the excluded *is* the fundamental antagonism rupturing capitalism today (and hence crucial to the idea of communism). Žižek recognizes that the focus on exclusion easily elides with "the liberal-tolerant-multicultural topic of 'openness'... at the expense of a properly Marxist notion of social antagonism."[30] Yet he argues that the inclusion of the proletariat is an inclusion of a different sort, an inclusion of capitalism's point of

30   Slavoj Žižek, *First as Tragedy, Then as Farce*, London, Verso: 2009, 100.

symptomal exclusion ("part of no part") that effectively dismantles it.

A lot rides on the notion of "proletariat" here, as my discussion of the changes in capitalism attests. On the one hand, Žižek rightly detaches "proletarian" from the factory, treating *proletarianization* as a process that deprives humans of their "substance" and reduces them to pure subjects. On the other, he identifies exclusion as a particular kind of proletarianization, one by which some are made directly to embody "substance-less subjectivity." They are the material remainders of the system, its unavoidable and necessary byproducts. Because the entire system relies on their exclusion (or their inclusion as remainders)—because they embody the truth that capitalism produces human refuse, surplus populations with no role or function—to include them would destroy the system itself.

Žižek's argument is most compelling when it conceives proletarianization as a process. Yet his rendering of proletarianization as a form of exclusion (rather than exploitation) obscures the necessary and productive role of proletarianization for capital, the way that proletarianization is a form of capitalism's capture and inclusion of human labor. As Marx describes in

Capital, the violent process of primitive accumulation provides capital with the workers it needs.

Neoliberalism (with its declining investment in production and diversion of capital into finance) amplifies the process of proletarianization. For example, economists David Autor and David Dorn describe a polarization of employment in so-called advanced economies over the last thirty years. The numbers of highly-skilled jobs have increased (Autor and Dorn do not discuss where these jobs are). Middle-skill, middle-class jobs have steadily declined, as have low-skill, non-service sector jobs. At the same time, low-skill, low-wage service sector jobs have ballooned. So there are decreasing numbers of jobs in mining, assembling, operating, and transporting and substantially increasing (53 percent between 1980 and 2005) numbers of jobs in childcare, hairdressing, food service, home health care, cleaning, and gardening. Autor and Dorn attribute the rise of this service sector to the widespread adoption of computing technologies. They write, "As the declining price of computer technology has driven down the wage paid to routine tasks, low skill workers have reallocated their labor supply to service occupations, which are difficult to automate because they rely

heavily on dexterity, flexible interpersonal communication and direct physical proximity."[31] "Reallocation"
points to proletarianization, that is, to capitalism's
production and consumption of the workers it needs.

Žižek's merger of proletarianization with the part-
of-no-part is one-sided in its restricted focus on the
discarded proletarian and omission of the productive
(of services as well as goods) proletariat. Like the
ancient *demos* Rancière describes, Žižek's proletariat
is characterized by freedom. In Žižek's version, the
proletariat, as part-of-no-part, lacks "the particular
features that would legitimate their place within the
social body—they belong to the set of society without
belonging to any of its subsets."[32] This proletariat is
free in the sense of free-floating, not constrained within
a given place, undetermined by features that situate
it. Yet as Marx explains in *Capital*, the freedom of the
worker is the form of dependence on capital, the worker's
inclusion within the capitalist system. The bourgeois
state recognizes this inclusion: from the standpoint of

31   David Autor and David Dorn, "The Growth of Low Skill
Service Jobs and the Polarization of the U.S. Labor Market,"
April 2012, econ-www.mit.edu/files/1474.
32   Slavoj Žižek, *In Defense of Lost Causes*, 413.

the state, the individual worker is equal to the individual capitalist; both are free to choose whether to contract one with the other.

An additional difficulty stems from treating contemporary communicative capitalism as if it were a whole marked by a constitutive exclusion where that exclusion designates persons as a part-of-no-part. As Boltanski and Chiapello outline, the inclusion/exclusion binary today designates a relation not to a whole but to a network.[33] The excluded are those who are vulnerable because they are disconnected; they lack links to networks of opportunity, security, and sustenance. In a network model, there are no symptomal points, no points the inclusion of which destroys the entire system. There are just more links. Links can be added or dropped with little impact on the network form. Admittedly, networks can experience overload, instances of self-organized criticality where they disintegrate and collapse. But an image of network overload is not the same as that of a whole and its constitutive exclusion, particularly insofar as networks can often route around breakdowns.

33 Luc Boltanski and Eve Chiapello, *The New Spirit of Capitalism*, trans. Gregory Elliott, London: Verso, 2007.

Networks, particularly the mass, rapid, affective networks of contemporary communicative capitalism, present the particular problem of holding onto, keeping open, the gap of desire. Immediate demands to upload, share, and search, as well as the easy absorption of political activity into the circuits of participatory media, format lack as loss, sublimating it and dispersing it back into the everyday. The displacement of political conflict to the terrain of networked media has the perverse repercussion of perpetually expanding the topography of struggle even as it constantly signals the locations, intentions, and associations of those who are fighting. Thus far, this expansion has strengthened communicative capitalism as it feeds on accelerating crises and emergencies. It also increases the exposure and vulnerability of those engaged in active protest and resistance on the ground.[34]

If the people as the rest of us are the subject of communism and sovereignty is our collective steering of our common resources and conditions, how should this control be understood? In the following chapters, I take

34 See my discussion in *Blog Theory*, Cambridge: Polity, 2010.

up this question in connection with the productivity of the communicative common and the organizational role of the party. In the remainder of this chapter, I consider Peter Hallward's provocative defense of voluntarism. Once the historical determinism of the merger narrative is no longer convincing and neither the unity nor the interest of the broad class of working people can be taken as given, is voluntarism the best available way to conceive collective political will?

Developing a line of thought offered by Badiou, Hallward argues against contemporary theory's widespread rejection of voluntarism to affirm the "dialectical voluntarism" of the will of the people. *Contra* those who would devalue self-determination and self-emancipation as they privilege "various forms of either indetermination (the interstitial, the hybrid, the ambivalent, the simulated, the undecidable, the chaotic ...) or hyperdetermination ('infinite' ethical obligation, divine transcendence, unconscious drive, traumatic repression, machinic automation)," he advocates a broadly Rousseauian or Jacobin account of the general will as the political will of a mobilized people. By "will," Hallward means the excess of practical freedom over the given or feasible: "To affirm the primacy of the prescriptive will is to insist that in politics all external forms of determination ... are nonetheless secondary." By "people" he means "those who, in any given situation, formulate, assert, and sustain a fully common (and thus fully inclusive and egalitarian) interest, over and above any divisive or exclusive interest." "Will of the people" thus designates "a deliberate, emancipatory, and inclusive process of collective self-determination. Like any kind of will, its exercise is voluntary and autonomous, a matter of practical freedom; like any form of collective action, it involves assembly and organization."[35]

The dialectical component of Hallward's voluntarism appears in the relationship between people and will. Hallward does not treat the people as an empirical designation for the inhabitants of a particular territory, the citizens of a particular nation, or the occupants of a particular social class. Rather, he conceives them through their active willing, that is, their active identification with an emergent general interest. Like Rousseau, Hallward differentiates between the will that is general

35   Peter Hallward, "The Will of The People: Notes Toward a Dialectical Voluntarism," *Radical Philosophy* 155, 2009, 17–30.

in terms of its common, egalitarian interest and a will that is partial or particular (non-generalizable). "Will" and "people," then, are mutually determining.

Insofar as the people are those who formulate, assert, and sustain a fully common interest, they exceed any immediate assemblage of people, any given movement or event. Formulation, assertion, and sustenance, in other words, point to the broader traditions and practices Hegel associates with ethical life and Marx treats as material factors in histories of struggle. If the people are those who formulate, assert, and sustain a fully common interest, then included among them are those who have thought and created, fought and died in the service of this interest. They are the people who could be and who we could have been. The people manifest themselves in signifying stresses, gaps, and ruptures, in the force of an absence, as much as they do in their presence.

The people likewise manifest themselves in concrete political association, which is why institutions and practices are sites of struggle. Since institutions and practices are and can be manifestations of the will of the people, vehicles for its determination and expression, such a will cannot be understood as fully transparent, known, or even voluntary. Irreducible to the conscious choice of individuals, it animates a broader subjectivity that is also a locus of struggle. We can say, then, that the general will designates a structure of desire: a necessary gap in the people mobilized in and for the collective. The conflict between common and particular interest doesn't end; it isn't resolved once and for all. It is a movement and process that requires the ongoing work of clarification, concentration, and organization.

The people as a divisive political subject produces itself through its practices. Its will precedes not only its knowledge of what is willed, but the people itself. The people are willing even if the content of that will cannot be understood in terms of a specific demand. Insofar as the general will is inseparable from (although not reducible to) the practices that sustain it, the new practices of occupation and assembly, their break with the everyday, suggest a people in the process of reformatting itself, trying to make itself think, do, and desire otherwise. Barricades, occupations, strikes, hacks, boycotts, and demonstrations work on the people who will them perhaps even more than on their opponents. Yet the recession of these enactments of popular will back into habits that affirm and reinforce communicative capitalism suggests the continued willing of the previous actualization of the conflict between general and particular, that is, the ongoing and persistent challenge of the general will. Falling back into the given and familiar is easy, sometimes catching us unawares: we start to think we are doing something new only to realize that capitalism shares our fascination with novelty. Desire can be sublimated into drive. Momentary struggles are nonetheless not pointless: their signifying stresses remain and the practice of inscribing, remembering, and interpreting them helps formulate, assert, and sustain a common egalitarian interest. The challenge, insofar as we constitute the practices that constitute us, is in the development of enduring forms of egalitarian association through which we can make ourselves into the people we want to be.

Hallward's dialectical voluntarism suggests an understanding of the sovereignty of the people in terms of a collective egalitarian universalist desire. Because the active, willing people are not identical to the passive, individualized population, and because the desire for the collective and egalitarian necessarily exceeds any given set of institutions and practices, sovereignty provides a better name for the rule of the people than dictatorship. Historically, dictatorship has denoted a temporary arrangement. Whether as a provision in the Roman constitution or a step toward the withering away of the state, dictatorship marks the exceptional convergence of legality and illegality, force and right. Its limited temporality, suggestive of emergency measures and states of exception, allows for acts committed outside of relations of accountability, acts justified by revolutionary fervor alone. As exceptions, they contribute to excessive rather than unavoidable violence. Excess merges with situation. It is better for the violence of rule to remain exceptional, wrong, and nonetheless in need of justification: was it necessary or was it driven by vengeance, enjoyment, particularity? Did it serve the common good? And even if it did, can its justification be generally willed? The revolutionary fury of the people is without limit or control. But this cannot and should not be incorporated in a governing or constitutional form (whether dictatorship of the proletariat or sovereignty of the people). Doing so invites and permits excessive measures in the name of revolutionary change, as if transforming the people were a process that could end.

The rule of the people is unsurpassable. The forms it takes necessarily vary—the sovereignty of the people does not have to be only or exclusively in the form of state sovereignty. State sovereignty is likewise limited, provisional, and incomplete insofar as the people exceed state forms. But only in a world without people would there be no need for the rule of the people. This rule can be thought in terms of self-governance, self-control, self-steering. Then it can and must be combined and thought with the trans-subjective, mutually determining conditions of selves, such that there is no self-governance absent collective self-governing. Marx's description of communism as the free development of each compatible with the free development of all expresses this mutual determination or dialectical voluntarism. Absent the collective determination of the people over their conditions, each remains unfree.

This is the sense designated by the sovereignty of the people as the rest of us. Insofar as communism names this sovereignty, communist movement strives to bring the conditions for it into being, grasping that these conditions are material and that the political sovereignty of the people is impossible when the basic conditions of our lives are outside of our collective determination.

To reiterate, this sovereignty is unavoidably partial and incomplete. Important determinants of our lives—when we are born, when we die, who our parents are, who we love, our mother tongue, the weather—remain outside our determination. We do well to remain mindful of sovereignty's limits. Yet these limits do not mean that other determinants are similarly outside our attempts to steer them. We can and already do make decisions about who gets what, who has what, what is rewarded, what is punished, what is amplified, what is thwarted. To this extent, securing the conditions of possibility for our sovereignty over ourselves as the people, the conditions that keep communist desire alive, necessarily brings about additional limits to sovereignty—it cannot dissolve its own conditions of possibility and remain sovereign.

Chapter Four

Common and Commons

Communism tags a fourth feature of our contemporary setting: the ideas of the common and the commons. Michael Hardt uses the notion of the *common* to draw out the specificity of the neoliberal assault on the people. For Hardt, neoliberalism is more than a policy entailing the privatization of public property and services. It is a seizure of what is common—knowledge, language, images, and affects.[1] Slavoj Žižek emphasizes the *commons* insofar as reference to the commons "justifies the resuscitation of the notion of communism: it enables us to see the progressing 'enclosure' of the commons as a process of proletarianization of those who are thereby excluded from their own substance."[2] As I explained in chapter three, a

1   Michael Hardt, "The Common in Communism," in *The Idea of Communism*, ed. Costas Douzinas and Slavoj Žižek, London: Verso, 2010, 136.
2   Slavoj Žižek "How to Begin from the Beginning," in *The Idea of Communism*, 213. In contrast, Nick Dyer-Witheford

benefit of the concept of proletarianization is that it turns our attention away from empirical classes and toward the processes of dispossession accompanying capital accumulation. Here I consider the processes of exploitation and expropriation specific to communicative capitalism. The concepts of the common and the commons contribute to this account as they highlight not only new experiences of collectivity but also barriers to the politicization of these experiences.

Hardt's conception of language, ideas, knowledge, and affects as themselves already common occludes antagonism. It proceeds as if we did not speak multiple, incommensurable languages, as if referents and systems of meaning didn't clash with one another, as if knowledges did not emerge in and through conflict. But if antagonism is a constitutive feature of human experience, should we deny it? Or should we claim it, occupy it, and force it in one direction rather than another? Which is the better approach for communists today: repeating in our contemporary setting the epic

positions the common as an alternative to a communism reduced to a "centralized command economy and a repressive state." See his "Commonism," in *What Would It Mean to Win?*, ed. Turbulence Collective, Oakland, CA: PM Press, 2010, 106.

and never-ending struggle of workers against owners, many against few, or appealing to the potentiality of capacities we all share, capacities of language, communication, and thought?

If antagonism is an irreducible feature of our setting, then division is common to communication. Division goes all the way down, separating speaker from utterance, utterance from meaning, and meaning from hearer, audience, recipient. What resonates to one, what is available as a resource for thinking and relating to others, is always already distanced, dissipated, or bracketed—whether temporally, tribally, topically, or topographically. Communication is necessarily partial, filled with holes, inseparable from power and hierarchy, reliant on exclusion. Communicative capitalism mobilizes these parts and holes, these fragments in motion, filling them in with images and feelings and bits of enjoyment. Free-floating words and images are mashed up and recombined, recirculated and redeployed, the fact of their transmission displacing previous models of message and response. How many page views? How many copies sold? The magnitude, the surplus of contributions, accumulates in data banks on server farms, potential information for spies and ad-men as soon as the quants and geeks figure out how to value it and put it to use. Perpetually engaged, we search and link, making the paths we follow—even as Google claims the traces as its own. We constitute the practices that constitute us. We collectively determine our collective conditions, but not yet as the people, still as populations.

I begin with a brief sketch of the relationship between neoliberalism and communicative capitalism. Understood most broadly, neoliberalism designates a particular strategy of class domination that uses the state to promote certain competitive dynamics for the benefit of the very rich. In Duménil's and Lévy's words, "Neoliberalism is a new stage of capitalism that emerged in the wake of the structural crisis of the 1970s. It expresses the strategy of the capitalist classes in alliance with upper management, specifically financial managers, intending to strengthen their hegemony and expand it globally."[3] Less a strategy for production than for the transfer of wealth to the very

3   Gérard Duménil and Dominique Lévy, *The Crisis of Neoliberalism*, Cambridge, MA: Harvard University Press, 2011, 1.

rich, neoliberalism places the "needs of money ... over those of production."[4] Pursued through policies of privatization, deregulation, and financialization, and buttressed by an ideology of private property, free markets, and free trade, neoliberalism has entailed cuts in taxes for the rich and cuts in protections and benefits for workers and the poor, resulting in an exponential increase in inequality.

Communicative capitalism is an ideological formation wherein capitalism and democracy converge in networked communication technologies. Ideals of access, inclusion, discussion, and participation take material form in the expansion and intensification of global telecommunications. Changes in information networks associated with digitalization, speed, and storage capacity accelerate and intensify elements of capitalism and democracy, consolidating the two into a single ideological formation.[5]

4   Doug Henwood, *Wall Street*, London: Verso, 1998, 237.
5   For more on communicative capitalism, see my *Publicity's Secret*, Ithaca, NY: Cornell University Press, 2002; *Blog Theory*, Cambridge, UK: Polity, 2010; and the first chapter of *Democracy and Other Neoliberal Fantasies*, Durham, NC: Duke University Press, 2009.

The relation between neoliberalism and communicative capitalism is historical and contingent. In principle, a convergence between capitalist and democratic ideals in networked communications could have accompanied Keynesian economic policies. In actuality, neoliberalism and communicative capitalism have been mutually reinforcing. Networked information technologies have been the means through which people have been subjected to the competitive intensity of neoliberal capitalism. Enthusiastically participating in personal and social media—*I have broadband at home! My new tablet lets me work anywhere! With my smartphone, I always know what's going on!*—we build the trap that captures us, a trap which extends beyond global use of mobile phones and participation in social networks to encompass the production of these phones and the hardware necessary to run these networks.

Investment in information technologies drove the nineties dot-com bubble, feeding New Economy hype, generating excess capacity, and leading to no discernible increase in productivity apart from that in the high-tech industry. Even after the bubble burst, New Economy rhetoric continued to extol digitalization for enabling capitalism to overcome its contradictions.

Doug Henwood indicts this discourse for appealing to utopian impulses in anti-utopian times: "Find capitalism too controlling? No, it's spontaneous! Too inegalitarian and exploitative? No, it overturns hierarchies! Vulgar, brutal, de-skilling, and mercenary? *Au contraire*, it's creative and fun! Unstable? Nah, that's just its miraculous dynamism at work!"[6]

Widely celebrated for making work fun, inspiring creativity, and opening up entrepreneurial opportunities, networked information and communication technology contributed to the production of new knowledge-based enterprises. Its more pronounced legacy, however, has been widespread de-skilling, surveillance, and the acceleration and intensification of work and culture: the freedom of "telecommuting" quickly morphed into the tether of 24/7 availability, permanent work. Describing a key contradiction of communicative capitalism, Franco Berardi writes, "If you want to survive you have to be competitive and if you want to be competitive you must be connected, receive and process continuously an immense and growing mass of data," and hence under constant soul-destroying pressure to

6   Doug Henwood, *After the New Economy*, New York: The New Press, 2005, 37.

keep up, stay alert, remain motivated.[7] Communication technologies made capitalism acceptable, exciting, and cool, immunizing it from critique by rendering critics into outmoded technophobes. At the same time, these technologies provided the basic components neces- sary for neoliberalism's acceleration of capitalism, not to mention a bunch of super-fun diversions enabling people to feel radical and connected while playing on their laptops.

Communication technologies contribute to the dis- placement and dispersion of critical energy such that even as inequality has intensified, forming and organizing a coherent opposition has remained a per- sistent problem—and this in a setting lauded for the way it provides everyday people with new capacities for involvement. Participatory media is personalizing media, not only in the sense of surveillance and track- ing but also in the sense of the injunction to find out for oneself and share one's opinion. Ubiquitous personal communications media turn our activity into passivity, capturing it and putting it into the service of capital- ism. Angry, engaged, desperate to do *something*, we

7   Franco Berardi, *Precarious Rhapsody*, New York: Minor Compositions, 2009, 42.

look for evidence, ask questions, and make demands. Yet the information we need to act seems perpetually out of reach; there is always something we misunderstand or do not know.

The astronomical increases in information that our searching, commenting, and participating generate entrap us in a setting of communication without communicability. As contributions to circuits of information and affect, our utterances are communicatively equivalent; their content, their meaning, is unimportant. On a blog, for example, gibberish written by an automated bot is as much a comment as any thoughtful reflection. The specific contribution has no symbolic efficiency; rather, it marks only the fact of its having been made. This decline in a capacity to transmit meaning, to symbolize beyond a limited discourse or immediate, local context, characterizes communication's reconfiguration into a primarily economic form. It produces for circulation, not use. As Hardt and Negri argue in *Empire*, communication "is the form of capitalist production in which capital has succeeded in submitting society entirely and globally to its regime."[8] Having become

8   Michael Hardt and Antonio Negri, *Empire*, Cambridge, MA: Harvard University Press, 2000, 347.

production, communication flows and circulates with little to no regard for transmitting meaning. Channeled through cellular networks and fiber-optic cables, onto screens and into sites for access, storage, retrieval, and counting, communication merges with the capitalist circuits it produces and amplifies.

Capitalist productivity derives from its expropriation and exploitation of communicative processes. This does not mean that information technologies have replaced manufacturing; in fact, they drive a wide variety of mining, chemical, and biotechnological industries. Nor does it mean that networked computing has enhanced productivity outside the production of networked computing itself. Rather, it means that capitalism has subsumed communication such that communication does not provide a critical outside. Communication serves capital, whether in affective forms of care for producers and consumers, the mobilization of sharing and expression as instruments for "human relations" in the workplace, or contributions to media circuits.[9]

Marx's analysis of value in *Capital* helps explain how communication can be a vehicle for capitalist

9   Eva Illouz, *Cold Intimacies*, Cambridge, UK: Polity, 2007.

subsumption. Value, for Marx, derives from the social character of labor. What is common to different kinds of human labor is that they are all labor in the abstract, components of the larger homogeneous mass of human labor. Products of labor are "crystals of this social substance, common to them all," that is to say, values.[10] Communicative capitalism seizes, privatizes, and attempts to monetize the social substance. It doesn't depend on the commodity-thing. It directly exploits the social relation at the heart of value. Social relations don't have to take the fantastic form of the commodity to generate value for capitalism. Via networked, personalized communication and information technologies, capitalism has found a more straightforward way to appropriate value.

One of the clearest expressions of communicative capitalism's direct exploitation of the social substance is Metcalfe's Law: "The value of a communications network is proportional to the square of the number of its users."[11] The basic idea is that the more people

10 Karl Marx, *Capital* (abridged), ed. David McLellan, New York: Oxford University Press, 2008, 15.
11 Bob Briscoe, Andrew Odlyzko, and Benjamin Tilly, "Metcalfe's Law is Wrong," July 2006, spectrum.ieee.org.

using a network, the more valuable it is. Although not an accurate rendition of Robert Metcalfe's (inventor of Ethernet) actual argument, the law named for him became Silicon Valley gospel, in part because it was widely and enthusiastically preached by Republican entrepreneur George Gilder, becoming one of the core beliefs anchoring claims for the New Economy. During the dot-com boom, venture capitalists and internet entrepreneurs invoked Metcalfe's law like a mantra because it seemed to reveal the secret to success expressed in their vernacular of "'network effects,' 'first-mover advantage,' 'Internet time,' and, most poignant of all, 'build it and they come.'"[12] There are multiple problems with Metcalfe's Law, including those of scale (larger networks may be more prone to crashes and delays) and the suppositions regarding the relations between the links (that all are active, say). More important is the fact that so many dot-com startups failed: there is a gap between the value of a network and the monetization of that value. The capitalists didn't know how to turn value into profit.

Nonetheless, the truth in Metcalfe's Law is its association of value with the communicative network itself.

12   Ibid.

If the Web were just a bunch of pages, it would not have the value it has today. "It is precisely because every Web page can, in principle, link to any other page that the Web has grown as it has."[13] Value is a property of the relations, the links, between and within pages. Google's PageRank algorithm, for example, is one of the most successful information retrieval algorithms because it takes linking into account. John Markoff, in the business section of the *New York Times*, explains that "the basic technology that made Google possible, known as 'PageRank,' systematically exploits human knowledge and decisions about what is significant to order search results."[14] For Markoff, what's interesting about PageRank and other such algorithms is their "extraordinary" potential for profit—they mine and extract common knowledge. The same point can be rendered critically: networked communications are the form of capitalism's subsumption of the social substance to its terms and dynamics. Matteo Pasquinelli thus argues

13   James Hendler and Jennifer Golbeck, "Metcalfe's Law, Web 2.0, and the Semantic Web," cs.umd.edu.
14   John Markoff, "Entrepreneurs See a Web Guided by Common Sense," *New York Times*, November 12, 2006, nytimes.com.

that "Google is a parasitic apparatus of capture of the value produced by common intelligence."[15] He treats the prestige that PageRank attends to (and reflexively enhances) in terms of the "network value" of any given link. "Network value" describes a link's social relations: How many other links is it related to? Are those links related to other links? How many? Google captures this value, the link's social substance, its place within a general system of social relations.

Communication in communicative capitalism joins together the communicative equivalence of contributions with the inequality of their network value. Rather than a setting where a speaker delivers a message to a hearer who has to first consider matters of intent and intelligibility (*why is she telling me this and does it make sense?*), communicative capitalism is one where messages are contributions to a circulating flow of inputs. As contributions, messages are communicatively equivalent; their content, meaning, and intent is irrelevant. Yet this equivalence is accompanied by dynamic hierarchies and real inequality, a

15   Matteo Pasquinelli, "Google's PageRank Algorithm: A Diagram of the Cognitive Capitalism and the Rentier of the Common Intellect," matteopasquinelli.com.

contradiction perhaps best expressed as "some contributions are more equal than others"—because of their links. Google search results tell us that networks recognize inequality. Money and influence make a difference. Results can be paid for, manipulated for a price. The already prominent and popular, the corporate friendly and media savvy, beat out the small and rare, a phenomenon I discuss below in terms of powerlaws. What matters here is that the contradiction between equivalence and inequality in communicative contributions repeats the "secret of the expression of value" that Marx describes in connection with commodities. Equality in circulation rests on a dominant relation of exploitation.

We learn from Marx that increases in commodity production result in the loss of value of any given commodity. Capitalism as commodity production comes up against this limit. The very drive to produce more results in the diminution of the value of production. It's no surprise that a globally unleashed capitalism would encounter the loss of an incentive to make things, that is, a decline in the willingness of capital to invest in the production of goods. In response, it has found unique ways to exploit the social substance, ways deeply imbricated with communicative capitalism's injunctions to connect, participate, and share.

Cesare Casarino treats the self-reproducing excess of contemporary capitalism in terms of the common. For him, "common" is neither an attribute nor a thing. Like capitalism itself, the common is a dynamic process. It is production. Glossing Hardt and Negri, Casarino writes, "nowadays the common is virtually indistinguishable from that which continually captures it, namely, capital understood as a fully—that is, intensively and extensively—global network of social relations."[16] Casarino distinguishes this sense of the common as a global network of social relations from the idea of the commons. The commons is *finite* and characterized by *scarcity*. In contrast, the common is *infinite* and characterized by *surplus*. The common thus designates and takes the place of human labor power (Marx's source of value), now reconceived in the broadest possible terms of the potential of creativity, thought,

16 Cesare Casarino, "Surplus Common," *In Praise of the Common: A Conversation On Philosophy and Politics*, Cesare Casarino and Antonio Negri, Minneapolis, MN: University of Minnesota Press, 2008, 15.

knowledge, and communication as themselves always plural, open, and productive.

Both common and commons are material and immaterial, natural and historical. Although the common indicates language, affect, thought, and knowledge— that is, communication—it is not detached from its materiality and historicity. Casarino thereby clarifies what the term "immaterial labor" tends to occlude. Communication depends on a complex assemblage: satellites, fiber-optic cables, broad spectrum bandwidth, cellular networks, SIM cards, laptops, mobile phones, personal media devices, screens, protocols, code, software, search engines, radio signals, blogs, images, emotions, catch phrases, jingles, jargon, citations, archives, fears, omissions, comfort, denial. Installing breaks in this assemblage on the basis of an always questionable materiality closes off what the present opens, namely, the fecundity of communicative substance.

The move from commons to common helps explain exploitation and expropriation in contemporary capitalism. As Marx made clear, at least one of the problems with the expropriation of the *commons* is that a few get a lot and some are left with nothing, thus having to sell their labor power. Privatization leaves them deprived of what they had. A contemporary version of this deprivation occurs through the widespread extension of credit—whether in the form of subprime mortgages, student loans, high-interest credit cards, or leverage in investment banking. Such forms of credit privatize the future as they deprive the indebted of what they will have. The *common* is different. There is expropriation, but an expropriation that does not appear to leave many with little. There is more than enough, perhaps even too much. A question for the capture of the common in capitalism, then, is the crime or harm: If there is abundance or surplus, why is expropriation a problem? Or is the problem some kind of exploitation, and if so, what kind?

Networked communications provide multiple instances of expropriation and exploitation of the common. Here are six: data, metadata, networks, attention, capacity, and spectacle. Each of these is an interconnected yet distinct exploitation of the social substance. The notion of the common, with and against the idea of the commons, enables this exploitation to appear as exploitation. In other words, it enables us to grasp the precise ways in which communicative capitalism runs up against its own contradictions.

First, Facebook and Amazon, like many internet companies, claim ownership of information placed on their sites. They claim as their own property the products of unremunerated creative, communicative labor. Profiting from the voluntary and unpaid labor of millions, they extend into society exploitative practices already coincident with networked communications. Google wouldn't have started without free software— it relied originally on the Linux kernel. Building it from scratch would have taken 270 developers roughly eleven years and cost 431 million dollars.[17]

A second kind of expropriation is of our metadata— our search patterns, friends, and relationships. User desire to navigate a rich information field is exploited for the access it provides to the larger field of choices and links. As we already saw in Pasquinelli's account of network value, Google treats the traces left by searching and linking as its own potential resource to mine and market.

A third version of expropriation and exploitation of the social substance reiterates the division within the

17 I owe this point to Marcell Mars, personal communication.

people, exposing this division as a matter of exploitation rather than exclusion. I call this network exploitation. It involves the structure of complex networks.

Complex networks are characterized by free choice, growth, and preferential attachment. Examples include academic citation networks, the popularity of blogs and websites, as well as blockbuster movies and bestsellers, all of which can be explained in terms of powerlaws. As Albert-László Barabási demonstrates, complex networks follow a powerlaw distribution of links. The item in first place or at the top of a given network has twice as many links as the item in second place, which has more than the one in third and so on, such that there is very little difference among those at the bottom but massive differences between top and bottom. So lots of novels are written. Few are published. Fewer are sold. A very few become bestsellers. Or lots of articles are written. Few are read. The same four are cited by everybody. The idea appears in popular media as the 80/20 rule, the winner-take-all or winner-take-most character of the new economy, and the "long tail."

In these examples, the common is the general field out of which the one emerges. Exploitation consists in efforts to stimulate the creative production of the field in the interest of finding, and then monetizing, the one. Expanding the field produces the one (or, hubs are an immanent property of complex networks). Such exploitation contributes to the expropriation of opportunities for income and paid labor, as in the collapse of print journalism and academic presses. We should recognize here a primary condition of labor under neoliberal capitalism. Now, rather than having a right to the proceeds of one's labor by virtue of a contract, ever more of us win or lose such that remuneration is treated like a prize. In academia, art, writing, architecture, entertainment, design, and increasing numbers of fields, people not only feel fortunate to get work, to get hired, to get paid, but ever more tasks and projects are conducted as competitions, which means that those doing the work are not paid unless they win. They work but only for a chance at pay.

Thomas Hobbes' description of merit is helpful here. In *Leviathan* (chapter fourteen), Hobbes explains that the one who performs first in the case of a contract *merits* that which he is to receive from the performance of the other. Because the first has performed (in accordance with the contract), the second is obliged to give the first what is due him. In the instance of a prize, we also say that the winner merits his winnings, but there is a difference: the prize is the product of the event, the contest. The relation between the one awarding the prize and the winner depends on the good will of the giver. Nothing specifically links the winner to the prize. The implication of this shift from contract to contest, from wages to prizes (a shift the consent to which is currently being manufactured in part via so-called reality television competitions), is the mobilization of the many to produce the one. Without the work of the many, there would not be one (who is necessarily contingent).

The administration of US President Barack Obama has made inducement prizes a key part of its "Strategy for American Innovation." Outlining its vision for a more competitive America, the White House announced that government "should take advantage of the expertise and insight of people both inside and outside" Washington by using "high-risk, high-reward policy tools such as prizes and challenges to solve tough problems."[18] What went unmentioned: the characteristics of those in a position to take risks. Contests

18 National Economic Council, "Strategy for American Innovation," whitehouse.gov.

privilege those who have the resources to take risks as they transfer costs associated with doing work to contestants (furthering neoliberalism's basic mechanism of socializing risk and privatizing reward). People pay to do work for which they will not be remunerated. It sounds like art, blogging, most writing, and most creative work. Work is done and then maybe paid for (the winner) and likely not (the losers).

In effect, each contestant faces the uncertainty typically associated with the capitalist who invests in production in the hope of realizing a profit. The difference is that rather than the outcome's being determined through competition in the market, the outcome of the contest is determined by a judge. The only link between the work and the remuneration comes from the prize giver, who is now in a position of judge, charitable giver, or beneficent lord and who has no obligation to any of the contestants. As a governmental policy, or approach to funding, the logic of the prize is extended into an acceptable work relation.

One might ask why inducement prizes are a problem: no one forces anyone to enter the competitions. The problem comes in with the shift in the approach to work, when prizes become a general practice. Those who don't choose to enter have fewer opportunities for contract-based work because the amount of contract-based work diminishes. The overall field changes such that people have little choice but to compete under these terms.

The next three instances of communicative expropriation and exploitation highlight the instability of the distinction between common and commons. These are attention, capacity, and spectacle.

The myriad entertainments and diversions available online, or as apps for smartphones, are not free. We don't usually pay money directly to Gmail, YouTube, Facebook, and Twitter. These don't cost money. They cost time. It takes time to post and write and time to read and respond. We pay with attention and the cost is focus.

Our attention isn't boundless. Our time is finite—even as we try to extract value out of every second (we don't have time to waste). We cannot respond to every utterance, click on every link, read every post. We have to choose even as the possibility of something else, something wonderful, lures us to search and linger. Demands on our attention, injunctions for us to communicate, participate, share—ever shriller and

more intense—are like so many speed-ups on the production line, attempts to extract from us whatever bit
of mindshare is left.

Berardi theorizes these speed-ups as a super-sat-
uration of attention: "The acceleration produced by
network technologies and the condition of precarious-
ness and dependence of cognitive labor, forced as it is
to be subject to the pace of the productive network, has
produced a saturation of human attention which has
reached pathological levels."[19] He connects increases
in depression, anxiety, panic disorder, suicide, and
the use of psycho-pharmaceuticals to this acceleration, as human psyches and brains come up against
their limits and oscillate between the hyper-excitation
of mobilized nervous energy and withdrawal and dis-
investment. Recent research in neuroscience confirms
that the incessant injunctions to find out, know, choose,
and decide are overloading and exhausting our basic
cognitive-emotional capacities. As a summary of this
research explained:

> No matter how rational and high-minded you try to
> be, you can't make decision after decision without

19   Berardi, *Precarious Rhapsody*, 71.

paying a biological price. It's different from ordinary physical fatigue—you're not consciously aware of being tired—but you're low on mental energy. The more choices you make throughout the day, the harder each one becomes for your brain, and eventually it looks for shortcuts, usually in either of two very different ways. One shortcut is to become reckless: to act impulsively instead of expending the energy to first think through the consequences. (Sure, tweet that photo! What could go wrong?) The other shortcut is the ultimate energy saver: do nothing. Instead of agonizing over decisions, avoid any choice.[20]

The communicative circuits of contemporary capitalism are loops of drive, impelling us forward and back through excitation and exhaustion. The more contributions we make, the more we expand the field in which others have to decide: respond or ignore? Either way a choice has to be made and the more choices one is compelled to make, the more exhausted one becomes.

When we respond to the invitations and incitements in our media feeds, whether as part of our work,

20 John Tierney, "Do You Suffer from Decision Fatigue?," *New York Times Magazine*, August 17, 2001.

our play, our activism, or our consumer practice, our contribution is an addition to an already infinite communicative field, a little demand on someone else's attention, a little incitement of an affective response, a digital trace that can be stored—and on and on and on. The cost of the exponentially expanding circuit of information and communication is particularly high for progressive and left political movements. Competition for attention—*how do we get our message across?*—in a rich, tumultuous media environment too often and easily means adapting to this environment and making its dynamic our own, which can result in a shift in focus from doing to appearing, that is to say, a shift toward thinking in terms of getting attention in the 24/7 media cycle and away from larger questions of building a political apparatus with duration. Infinite demands on our attention—demands we make on each other and which communicative capitalism captures and amplifies—expropriate political energies of focus, organization, duration, and will vital to communism as a movement and a struggle. It's no wonder that communicative capitalism is participationist: the more participation in networked media environments, the more traces to hoard and energies to capture or divert.

The limits of attention are not only the limits of individuals (and so can be resolved by distributing labor and crowdsourcing). They are the limits that make communication as such possible, as in, for example, distinctions between signal and noise as well as those characteristics of our habits, environments, and processes that direct our attention and thereby produce the circumstances of communication. The limits of attention are common. The common actualized in contemporary communication networks functions itself as a means of expropriation. Overproduction and overaccumulation of the common, then, are problems unique to communicative capitalism. As Christian Marazzi powerfully demonstrates, "the disproportion between the supply of information and the demand for attention is a *capitalistic* contradiction, an internal contradiction of the value form."[21]

The fact of attention's limits points to the division inseparable from communication: ideas and affects are not infinitely transferable, accessible, communicable. Hardt misses this when he argues that sharing ideas increases rather than decreases their "utility." He

21   Christian Marazzi, *Capital and Language*, trans. Gregory Conti, Los Angeles, CA: Semiotext(e), 2008, 141.

argues that "in order to realize their maximum productivity, ideas, images, and affects must be common and shared. When they are privatized their productivity reduces dramatically."[22] If productivity means "capacity to circulate" or "transmissibility into a variety of sectors," then increases in productivity (circulation) entail declines in specificity, accuracy, meaning, and registration. Present in ever wider and more differentiated settings, to ever more varied audiences, ideas change. This is part of the pleasure in mashing together video and audio clips—sounds and images take on new meanings, becoming something different from what they were before. Brands, logos, images, and identities lose their unique signifying capacity when they extend too broadly, to too many different items with too many different valences—which is exactly why corporations fight to keep them private. If everything is Nike, then Nike doesn't mean anything. To be clear: I'm not defending property rights in ideas and images. Rather, I am pointing out that it is not their privatization that fetters capitalist production but the opposite, namely, their proliferation into a massive,

22   Hardt, "The Common in Communism," 136.

circulating flow of increasingly valueless contributions insofar as each can command less and less attention. The contradiction is particular to communicative capitalism in that communication cannot be exponentially expanded as a form of capitalist production. It comes up against limits inherent to communication as such.

Casarino argues that potentiality is common. While potentiality is fully embedded within capitalism, it does not *belong* to capitalism. It doesn't belong to anybody. But Casarino moves too quickly to link potentiality to a common that exceeds capitalism's grasp. Communicative capitalism seizes excess, surplus, and abundance. Its drive impels us toward extra and more, new opportunities, unforeseen pleasures, chances, and risks that *if we don't take someone else will*, the very chances and risks that derivatives commodify and on which high finance speculates. Contemporary capitalism securitizes, monetizes, and privatives potential. It does so through the excessive generation of debt (whether of individuals, households, or states); through the amplified role of speculative finance in generating corporate profit; through the premediation of events such that massive amounts of energy and attention are focused on what could or might happen; and through the incitement of creative work toward producing the one.[23] Potential is the gap in the actual, the difference worth exploiting and betting on, as illustrated by the arbitrage and high-speed trades on which so many hedge funds rely.

The fifth instance of expropriation and exploitation of the common/commons involves capacities. Just as industrial labor expropriated craft skill, breaking it into its smallest components and distributing these components via mechanization and assembly lines, so does communicative capitalism participate in the dispossession of our previously common knowledge and capacities. Computer chips and processors, mobile phones and mp3 players are primary components of the expansion and acceleration of disposability. Computers are antiquated in under three years; mobile phones become old-fashioned (if not obsolete) in about eighteen months. We don't learn how to fix them, forgetting that this is something we once might have known. Capacities to repair items of daily use have also diminished. The supposition is that we can just buy a new one. Of course, this was already the case with the rapid

23   Richard Grusin, *Premediation: Affect and Mediality After 9/11*, New York: Palgrave Macmillan, 2010.

expansion of domestic goods after WWII. Middle class households in the US and UK became less likely to make the things they needed—clothes, furniture—and bought them instead. Pressures on households to earn income, even while raising kids and participating in the care of others, has meant increased reliance on take away, fast, and frozen food, with a corresponding decrease in capacities to prepare and cook fresh food. Contemporary popular culture highlights the expropriation of capacities that many in the middle and former middle class currently experience. Television experts provide guidance in household organization, basic cooking skills, and how to get along with others.

Neoliberal trends in higher education extend these dynamics to the university: in a society without skills, who needs a degree? Capitalism no longer requires a skilled, educated middle class, so mass university education is no longer necessary. It doesn't take as many people as we have to service the top 1 percent, so most of us are not needed any more (except as the field out of which the one can emerge). In a setting that reduces education to knowledge, knowledge to information, and information to data, we are told that we can find out anything we want to know by googling it.

In a nutshell: things do it for us so that we don't have to.[24] We don't need professors to tell us, or at least not very many—a couple of great universities can probably supply all the lawyers, scientists, bankers, and novelists a country needs (and if not, well, there is a global elite from which to draw). We've outsourced basic skills—or, they've been expropriated from us.

The sixth instance of exploitation and expropriation in communicative capitalism is spectacle. In *The Coming Community*, Giorgio Agamben presents the spectacle as "the extreme form of the expropriation of the Common." Through spectacle, we are dispossessed of the "very possibility of a common good." We are audience for, witnesses to, some dramatic event happening somewhere else to someone else. Yet insofar as the very appeal, the affective charge, of the spectacle is its mass quality, the way it makes us feel connected to a larger "we" to which we belong, the spectacle returns to us our linguistic nature in an inverted form. It exploits our aspirations for common being, uses them against us as a mode of communicative power through which we are held captive while a very few profit, and

24   See Gijs van Oenen, "Interpassive Agency," *Theory & Event* 14.2, 2011.

yet offers a glimpse of the possibility of a positivity that might be used against it.[25]

Agamben works from a dilemma expressed by Guy Debord: in the society of the spectacle, "the language of real communication has been lost" and a "new common language has yet to be found." Debord writes, "Spectacular consumption preserves the old culture in congealed form, going so far as to recuperate and rediffuse even its negative manifestations; in this way, the spectacle's cultural sector gives over expression to what the spectacle is implicitly in its totality—*the communication of the incommunicable*."[26] Agamben responds to the expropriation of communicativity that Debord identifies by turning the problem into the solution. He uses the spectacle against itself. The incommunicable dissolves the gap between the language lost and the language to be found. It can be communicated. Insofar as the incommunicable is common, it persists beyond even the most extreme attempts at its expropriation.

25 Giorgio Agamben, *The Coming Community*, trans. Michael Hardt, Minneapolis, MN: University of Minnesota Press, 1993.
26 Guy Debord, *The Society of the Spectacle*, trans. Donald Nicholson-Smith, New York: Zone Books, 1999, 133.

The spectacle thus contains its own overcoming. The expropriation of language in the spectacle opens up a new experience of language and linguistic being: "Not this or that content of language, but language *itself*, not this or that true proposition, but the very fact that one speaks."[27]

Agamben treats communication reflexively: he turns from *what* is said to *that* something is said. Not only is a negative condition (estrangement from linguistic being) treated as a positive opening (new experience of belonging), but its positivity is a result of reflexivity. Language turns on *itself*. Freud discusses drive as precisely this turning round upon the self, a turning that involves a shift from activity to passivity. Agamben finds positive potential in the communication of incommunicability by replacing the active aim of saying something with the passive fact of having said. The movement from commons to common repeats the shift from active to passive, from desire to drive. The force of scarcity that characterizes the *commons* pushes action, decision, a choice for this rather than that. The communicative excess, the surplus *common*, suggests

27 Agamben, *The Coming Community*, 83.

a field or milieu wherein activity has become passivity, a mode of capture or entrapment in the "not yet" or "perhaps." Social media take our ensemble of actions and return them to us as an endless communicative common. Generation is for circulation as our images and affects, opinions and contributions flow round and round, accumulating and distracting.

Hardt and Casarino appeal to an idea of the common as language, knowledge, and affect. They highlight what drives contemporary capitalism, what communicative capitalism expropriates and exploits. And they bring out emancipatory possibilities already present in our setting, in particular the common which exceeds its capture in capitalism and thereby holds out "the potential for an autonomous process that could destroy capital and create something entirely new." Hardt argues that "through the increasing centrality of the common in capitalist production—the production of ideas, affects, social relations and forms of life—are emerging the conditions and weapons for a communist project."[28] Insofar as each person is productive as an

28   Hardt, "The Common in Communism," 143.

expressive, feeling, communicating being and insofar as all are productive in their communicative interrelations—together we produce the social substance that constitutes us—any ownership or profit is clearly theft. Under communicative capitalism, such appropriation of the social substance is visible and undeniable—and thus a ground for arguments on behalf of global, guaranteed income: there is no one who does not contribute.

At the same time, however, the very communicative practices capitalism drives and exploits entrap us in circuits from which escape seems impossible: participation is personalization; the more we communicate, the less is communicated; expansions in expression and creativity produce the one rather than a collective of the many. The challenge, then, consists in breaking with current practices by insisting on and intensifying the division of and in the common. Continuing in the flow, persisting in the repetitions of drive, we over and over reconstitute capitalism's basic dynamic, perhaps generating "the possibility of another organization of social life" but also and at the same time hindering "that possibility from being realized."[29] Capitalism

29 Moishe Postone, "Rethinking Marx (in a Post-Marxist World)," obeco.no.sapo.pt/mpt.htm.

demands change, permanent revolution, crisis. Born out of opposition to planning, neoliberalism in particular thrives on shock and emergency, converging yet again with communicative capitalism in its mode of spectacle. To persist in the practices through which communicative capitalism exploits the social substance, then, is to fail to use division as a weapon on behalf of a communist project.

Division is common. We have to seize it.

Chapter Five

Desire

In a widely cited essay published in 1999, Wendy Brown uses Walter Benjamin's term "left melancholy" to diagnose a melancholia of the contemporary Left.[1] Her concern is with the fears and anxieties of a Left that is backward-looking, self-punishing, attached to its own failure, and seemingly incapable of envisioning an emancipatory egalitarian future. Timely and evocative, Brown's essay seemed to capture a truth about the end of a certain sequence of the North American, British, and European Left. Attuned to the ends and loss occasioned by the disintegration of the "we" previously held in common by the discourse of communism, Brown provided an opportunity to reflect on the failures and continuities in left projects in terms of the desires that sustain them. Her treatment of a "lost historical movement" thus suggested a kind

1 Wendy Brown, "Resisting Left Melancholy," *boundary 2* 26:3, 1999, 19–27.

of left "coming to grips" with the reality of neoliberal capitalism and the defeat of the welfare state.

Read from the distance of more than a decade, however, Brown's essay now appears to err in its basic account of what was lost and why. Her discussion of Benjamin is misleading. Her treatment of Freud is one-sided. Nonetheless, by analyzing the Left in terms of a general structure of desire, Brown opens up possibilities for reconceiving communist desire, possibilities this chapter extends as it outlines a fifth component of our contemporary setting that communism tags: a collective desire for collectivity.

"Left-Wing Melancholy" is the title of Benjamin's 1931 review of the poetry of Erich Kästner.[2] Kästner was a well-regarded poet, novelist, and journalist during the Weimar period. Benjamin describes Kästner's poetry as giving way to the complacency and fatalism of "those who are most remote from the processes of production and whose obscure courting of

2 Walter Benjamin, "Left-Wing Melancholy," trans. Ben Brewster, *Walter Benjamin, Selected Writings: 1931–1934*, volume 2, part 2, ed. Michael W. Jennings, Howard Eiland, and Gary Smith, Cambridge, MA: Harvard University Press, 1999, 423–27.

the state of the market is comparable to the attitude of a man who yields himself up entirely to the inscrutable accidents of his digestion."[3] In a further essay, "The Author as Producer," Benjamin uses Kästner as the exemplar of the "new objectivity," a literary movement that Benjamin argues "has made *the struggle against poverty* an object of consumption."[4] Quoting "a perceptive critic"—actually himself, writing in "Left-Wing Melancholy"—Benjamin says, "With the workers movement, this left-wing radical intelligentsia has nothing in common. It is, rather, a phenomenon of bourgeois decomposition ... The radical-left publicists of the stamp of Kästner, Mehring, or Tucholsky are the proletarian mimicry of decayed bourgeois strata. Their function is to produce, from the political standpoint, not parties but cliques; from the literary standpoint, not schools but fashions; from the economic standpoint, not producers but agents—agents or hacks who make a great display of their poverty, and a banquet out of

3 Ibid., 426.
4 Walter Benjamin, "The Author as Producer," trans. Edmund Jephcott, *Walter Benjamin, Selected Writings: 1931– 1934*, volume 2, part 2, ed. Michael W. Jennings, Howard Eiland, and Gary Smith, Cambridge, MA: Harvard University Press, 1999, 768–782.

yawning emptiness." As far as Benjamin is concerned, left-wing writers such as Kästner are hacks with no social function other than rendering the political situation into amusing content for public consumption. They transmit the apparatus of production rather than transform it, assimilating revolutionary themes into the bourgeois apparatus of production and publication while in no way placing in question the existence of the bourgeois class. Benjamin writes, "I define 'hack writer' as a writer who abstains in principle from alienating the productive apparatus from the ruling class by improving it in ways serving the interests of socialism."[5] In sum, Benjamin's critique in both "Left-Wing Melancholy" and "The Author as Producer" targets intellectual compromise, adaptation to the market, and the betrayal of the workers' movement, particularly insofar as this compromise, adaptation, and betrayal banks on and cans authentic revolutionary impulses already part of everyday proletarian life.

Brown claims that *"left melancholy* is Benjamin's unambivalent epithet for the revolutionary hack who is, finally, attached more to a particular political analysis or ideal—even to the failure of that ideal—than

5   Ibid., 776, 774.

to seizing possibilities for radical change in the present."[6] I disagree. Nowhere in his review of Kästner does Benjamin fault him for a lingering attachment to political ideals. Benjamin makes the opposite point, condemning Kästner for writing poems that are blind to action because "their beat very precisely follows the notes according to which poor rich folks play the blues." Benjamin describes Kästner's lyricism as protecting "above all the status interests of the middle stratum—agents, journalists, heads of departments… it noticeably abandons any striking power against the big bourgeoisie."[7] Kästner's melancholy is a trend, a commodity. He is not attached to an ideal; he has compromised revolutionary ideals by reducing them to consumer products.

Perhaps because her preoccupation is with the inadequacies of the contemporary Left, Brown does not emphasize the compromise of the left melancholic. Instead she reads Benjamin's critique of Kästner as suggesting that "sentiments themselves become things for the left melancholic who 'takes as much pride in the traces of former spiritual goods as the bourgeois do in

6   Brown, "Resisting Left Melancholy," 20.
7   Benjamin, "Left-Wing Melancholy," 426, 424.

their material goods.'" Brown locates in this reified loss a point of contact with the contemporary Left: "We come to love our left passions and reasons, our left analyses and convictions, more than we love the existing world that we presumably seek to alter with these terms or the future that would be aligned with them."[8] Benjamin, though, is not criticizing a Left for its attachment to left passions, reasons, analyses, and convictions. He is calling out Kästner and the "new objectivity" trend for their compromise and the resulting "metamorphosis of political struggle from a compulsory decision into an object of pleasure, from a means of production into an article of consumption."[9] Unlike Brown's, Benjamin's left melancholic sublimates left commitment to revolution and the proletariat, giving way to the bourgeois vision of the existing world instead of holding fast to revolutionary struggle.

Brown argues that "if the contemporary Left often clings to the formations and formulations of another epoch, one in which the notion of unified movements, social totalities, and class-based politics appeared to be viable categories of political and theoretical

8   Brown, "Resisting Left Melancholy," 21.
9   Benjamin, "Left-Wing Melancholy," 425.

analysis, this means that it literally renders itself a conservative force in history—one that not only mis-reads the present but installs traditionalism in the very heart of its praxis, in the place where commitment to risk and upheaval belongs."[10] In our present of unde-niable inequality, class war, and ongoing capitalist crisis, the necessity of unified movements and class-based analysis is undeniable in a way it perhaps was not when Brown was writing at the end of nineties. This clarity helps illuminate Benjamin's own position as opposite to the one Brown takes. His concern is not with a traditionalism at the heart of praxis but with the sublimation of left ideals in market-oriented writing and publishing. Unlike Brown's, Benjamin's left mel-ancholic is the one who gives in to "complacency and fatalism," ceding desire like the "satiated man who can no longer devote all his money to his stomach."[11]

The most valuable aspect of Brown's analysis comes when she turns to Freud's 1917 paper on melancholia to provide an account of a particularly left structure of desire. As is well known, Freud distinguishes melan-cholia from mourning. Mourning responds to the loss

10   Brown, "Resisting Left Melancholy," 25.
11   Benjamin, "Left-Wing Melancholy," 426.

of an object of love, whether that object is a person, country, freedom, or ideal.[12] Over the time of mourning, the subject painfully and piecemeal withdraws her attachment from the lost object. As in mourning, the melancholic subject presents an absence of interest in the outside world and a general inhibition of activity. The crucial difference is that the melancholic's lowering of self-regard is manifest in a self-reviling that extends to the very "over-coming of the instinct which compels every living thing to cling to life." The death drive, the force of loss, reformats the structure of desire itself. Freud writes, "The melancholic displays something else besides which is lacking in mourning—an extraordinary diminution in his self-regard, an impoverishment of his ego on a grand scale. In mourning it is the world which has become poor and empty; in melancholia it is the ego itself. The patient represents his ego to us as worthless, incapable of any achievement and morally despicable; he reproaches himself, vilifies himself and expects to

12 Sigmund Freud, "Mourning and Melancholia," *The Standard Edition of the Complete Psychological Works of Sigmund Freud, Volume XIV (1914–1916): On the History of the Psycho-Analytic Movement, Papers on Metapsychology and Other Works*, London: Hogarth Press, 1959, 237–58.

be cast out and punished."[13] To account for this difference in self-regard, Freud distinguishes between mourning's consciousness of loss and the unknown and unconscious dimension of object loss in melancholia. Something about the melancholic's loss remains unconscious. Even when the melancholic knows *that* he has lost, he does not know *what* he has lost, in what his loss consists for him. Psychoanalysis addresses this unconscious element of melancholic loss.

Freud accepts the melancholic subject's self-accusation—the subject really is weak, dishonest, petty, egoistic. Yet he notes that most of us, with our reasonably healthy neuroses, don't acknowledge these limitations. We try to hide these weaknesses from ourselves and others. The accuracy of the melancholic's self-description, then, is basically correct. Freud accepts it: "He [the subject] has lost his self-respect and he must have good reason for this."[14] The real question is why the subject has lost his self-respect, what the "good reason" for this loss is.

By way of an answer, Freud notes how in melancholia a critical agency splits off from the ego, a voice

13 Ibid., 245.
14 Ibid., 246.

of conscience that criticizes the poor ego for all its moral failings. He explains that clinical experience reveals that the specific criticisms the melancholic levels against himself correspond most fully not to the melancholic subject himself but to one whom the subject loves or should love: "The self-reproaches are reproaches against a loved object which have been shifted away from it on to the patient's own ego." What the patient seems to be saying about himself is really about someone else. The melancholic subject thus is one who has narcissistically identified himself with someone else, his loved object, now lost. Rather than acknowledging the loss, narcissistic identification protects the subject from it, bringing the object into the subject and enabling him to keep it as part of himself. This identification is fraught insofar as there is much about the loved object that the subject does not love—that the subject even hates. To deal with this unavowable hatred, a "special agency" of the ego splits off to judge and condemn the loved object, now part of the subject himself. Freud explains, "In this way an object loss was transformed into an ego-loss and the conflict between the ego and the loved person into a cleavage between the critical activity of the ego and

the ego as altered by identification."[15] The answer to
the question of the subject's loss of self-respect turns
on the object: it's the internalized object who is judged,
criticized, and condemned, not the subject at all.

Brown uses Freud's account of melancholia to
understand the fears and anxieties preventing the Left
from revising its anachronistic habits of thought. She
highlights the persistence of melancholic attachment
to a lost object, a persistence that, in superceding
conscious desires to recover, to move on, renders "melancholia a structure of desire, rather than a transient
response." She emphasizes as well the unconscious,
"unavowed and unavowable," nature of melancholic
loss. And she notes the shift of the "reproach of the
loved object" onto the left subject, a shift that preserves "the love or idealization of the object even as
the loss of this love is experienced in the suffering of
the melancholic." Recounting some of the many losses
on the Left—of local and international community, of a
moral and political vision capable of sustaining political work, of a historical moment—Brown asks whether
there might also be a still unconscious, unavowed
loss, namely, of "the promise that left analysis and

15   Ibid., 247, 248.

left commitment would supply its adherents a clear and certain path toward the good, the right, and the true."[16] She suggests that this promise formed the basis for left self-love and fellow feeling. So long as it remains foundational, unavowed and untransformed, it will doom the Left to self-destruction.

Freud's study of melancholia enables Brown to bring to light the disavowed attachment underlying the fierce debates over post-structuralism and the status of the subject characteristic of a particular mode of left theory. She asks, "What do we hate that we might preserve the idealization of that romantic left promise? What do we punish that we might save the old guarantees of the Left from our wrathful disappointment?"[17] Her answer is that hatred and punishment are symptoms, strikes we wage upon ourselves so as to preserve the promises and guarantees of left analysis. Scorn for identity politics and disparagement of discourse analysis, postmodernism, and "trendy literary theory" is the displaced form of narcissistic attachment to Marxist orthodoxy. It's an attack aimed at an interiorized object,

16   Brown, "Resisting Left Melancholy," 20, 21, 22.
17   Ibid., 22.

the loved and lost object that promised unity, certainty, clarity, and political relevance.

A benefit of Brown's discussion is its illumination of a certain fantasy in left desire: left melancholia extracts historical experiences of division, contestation, and betrayal from the Marxist tradition in theory and socialist states in practice. In their place it leaves an invincible, reified figure of the Master, one that is itself split between its authoritative and its obscene enactments. As Brown suggests, when leftists, stuck in their failure, blame this failure on post-structuralist theory and identity politics, they disavow the non-existence of such a Master. Clinging to an impossible, fantastic Marxism that never existed, they protect themselves from confronting the loss of its historical time, the end of the sequence beginning in 1917 or, perhaps, 1789. They shield themselves from the passing away of a time when it made sense to think in terms of the determinism of capital and the primacy of class.

Is Brown right? Having diagnosed left immobility and self-loathing as melancholic, does she correctly identify what was lost and what is retained, what is displaced and what is disavowed? And does her account of melancholia as a structure of desire exhaust the potential of her move to Freud, or might additional elements of his analysis also prove helpful for coming to grips with the Left and the force of loss?

Benjamin's account of left-wing melancholy suggests a loss of a different sort: the betrayal of revolutionary ideals, of the proletariat. He criticizes Kästner not only for clinging to a form marked by the depiction of the brutalities of everyday life but for commodifying this form, for packaging up the traces of spiritual goods as so much commercial content to be marketed and sold to the bourgeoisie. As Benjamin argues in "The Author as Producer," however revolutionary the political tendency associated with the "new objectivity" may appear, "it actually functions in a counterrevolutionary manner as long as the writer experiences his solidarity with the proletariat ideologically and not as a producer."[18] Attached to an ideological experience of solidarity, the left melancholic disavows his practice, the practical effect of his journalistic activities. What Brown construes as a real loss of socialist ideals for which the Left compensates via an obstinate and narcissistic attachment to a fantastic object, Benjamin presents as a compromise and betrayal that ideological

18   Benjamin, "The Author as Producer," 3.

identification with the proletariat attempts to displace. Brown suggests a Left defeated and abandoned in the wake of historical changes. Benjamin compels us to consider a Left that gave in, sold out.

Freud's gesture to the melancholic's loss of self-respect points in a similar direction. Describing a woman who "loudly pities her husband for being tied to such an incapable wife," Freud observes that she is really accusing her husband of incapacity. Her self-reproaches, some of which are genuine, "are allowed to obtrude themselves, since they help to mask the others and make recognition of the true state of affairs impossible." These reproaches, Freud writes, "derive from the pros and cons of the conflict of love that has led to the loss of love."[19] Might it not be the case that the woman rightly recognizes her inability to find a husband capable of sustaining her desire? Might she not be punishing herself for compromising, for making due, for allowing the pros and cons of the conflict of love to constrain her desire as she acquiesces to a reality of acceptance and moderation to which there seems to be no alternative? If the answer to these questions is "yes," then the woman's loss of self-respect is

19   Freud, "Mourning and Melancholia," 247.

an indication of the guilt she feels at having ceded her desire. To use the terms given to us by Lacan, "the only thing one can be guilty of is giving ground relative to one's desire."[20] The woman's identification with her husband is a compromise, the way she sublimates her desire so as to make him the object of it. The ferocity of her super-ego and the unrelenting punishment to which it subjects her indicates that she has given up on the impossibility of desire, desire's own constitutive dissatisfaction, to accommodate herself to everyday life.

Freud notes the delight the super-ego takes in torment as well as the fact that the subject enjoys it. He writes:

> If the love for the object—a love which cannot be given up though the object itself is given up—takes refuge in narcissistic identification, then the hate comes into operation on this substitutive object, abusing it, debasing it, making it suffer and deriving sadistic satisfaction from its suffering. The self-tormenting in melancholia, which is without doubt enjoyable, signifies, just like the corresponding

20 Jacques Lacan, *The Ethics of Psychoanalysis: The Seminar of Jacques Lacan, Book VII*, ed. Jacques-Alain Miller, trans. Dennis Porter, New York: Norton, 1997, 321.

phenomenon in obsessional neurosis, a satisfaction of trends of sadism and hate which relate to an object, and which have been turned round upon the subject's own self.[21]

Freud uses the terminology of the drives he sets out in "Instincts and Their Vicissitudes." As Lacan makes clear, what is crucial in the Freudian account of the drives is the way drive provides the subject with another way to enjoy. Unable to satisfy or maintain desire, the subject enjoys in another way, the way of the drive. Additionally, in contrast with desire, drive isn't a quest for a fantastic lost object; it's the force loss exerts on the field of desire. Drives don't circulate around a space that was once occupied by an ideal, impossible object. Rather, drive is the sublimation of desire as it turns back in on itself.

An emphasis on the drive dimension of melancholia, on Freud's attention to the way sadism in melancholia is "turned round upon the subject's own self," leads to an interpretation of the general contours shaping the Left that is different from Brown's. Instead of a Left attached to an unacknowledged orthodoxy, we have one that has

21   Freud, "Mourning and Melancholia," 250.

given way on the desire for communism, betrayed its historical commitment to the proletariat, and sublimated revolutionary energies into restorationist practices that strengthen the hold of capitalism. This Left has replaced commitments to the emancipatory, egalitarian struggles of working people against capitalism —commitments that were never fully orthodox, but always ruptured, conflicted, and contested—with incessant activity (like the mania Freud associates with melancholia) and so now satisfies itself with criticism and interpretation, small projects and local actions, particular issues and legislative victories, art, technology, procedures, and process. It sublimates revolutionary desire to democratic drive, to the repetitious practices offered up as democracy (whether representative, deliberative, or radical). Having already conceded to the inevitably of capitalism, it noticeably abandons "any striking power against the big bourgeoisie," to return to Benjamin's language. For such a Left, enjoyment comes from its withdrawal from responsibility, its sublimation of goals and responsibilities into the branching, fragmented practices of micropolitics, self-care, and issue awareness. Perpetually slighted, harmed, and undone, this Left remains stuck in repetition, unable to break out of the circuits of drive in which it is caught, unable because it enjoys them.

Might this not explain why such a Left confuses discipline with domination, why it forfeits solidarity in the name of an illusory, individualist freedom that continuously seeks to fragment and disrupt any assertion of collectivity and the common? The watchwords of critique within this structure of left desire are moralism, dogmatism, authoritarianism, and utopianism, watchwords enacting a perpetual self-surveillance: has an argument, position, or view inadvertently *risked* one of these errors? Even some of its militants reject party and state, division and decision, securing in advance an inefficacy sure to guarantee it the nuggets of satisfaction that drive provides.

If this Left is rightly described as melancholic—and I agree with Brown that it is—then its melancholia derives from the real existing compromises and betrayals inextricable from its history, its accommodations with reality, whether of nationalist war, capitalist encirclement, or so-called market demands. Lacan teaches that, like Kant's categorical imperative, the super-ego refuses to accept reality as an explanation for failure. Impossible is no excuse—desire is always impossible to satisfy. A wide spectrum of the contemporary Left has either accommodated itself, in one way or another, to an inevitable capitalism, or taken the practical failures of Marxism-Leninism to require the abandonment of antagonism, class, and revolutionary commitment to overturning capitalist arrangements of property and production. Melancholic fantasy—the communist Master, authoritarian and obscene—as well as sublimated, melancholic practices—there was no alternative—shield this Left, shield *us*, from confrontation with guilt over such betrayal as they capture us in activities that feel productive, important, radical.

Perhaps I should use the past tense here and say "shielded" because it seems more and more that the Left has worked or is working through its melancholia. While acknowledging the incompleteness of psychoanalysis's understanding of melancholia, Freud notes nonetheless that the unconscious work of melancholia comes to an end as "each single struggle of ambivalence" loosens "the fixation of the libido to the object" and the object is "abandoned as useless."[22] Freud's

22   Ibid., 255.

reference to "each single struggle of ambivalence" suggests that the repetitive activities I've associated with drive and sublimation might be understood more dialectically, that is, not merely as the form of accommodation but also as substantive practices of de- and reattachment, unmaking and making. Mladen Dolar and Slavoj Žižek emphasize this destructive dimension of the drive, the way its repetitions result in a clearing away of the old so as to make a space for the new.[23]

In a setting marked by a general acceptance of the end of communism and of particular political-theoretical pursuits in ethics, affect, culture, and ontology, a Left described in terms of its melancholic structure of desire may make less sense than a Left that doesn't exist at all. Brown's essay would then be a contribution to the working through and dismantling of left melancholia. In its place, multiple practices and patterns circulate within an academic-theoretical enterprise already subsumed within communicative capitalism. Some of the watchwords of anti-dogmatism remain, but their charge is diminished, replaced by more energetic attachment to new objects of inquiry and interest. The drive

23 Mladen Dolar, "Freud and the Political," *Theory & Event* 12.3, 2009.

shaping melancholia, in other words, is a force of loss as it turns round, fragments, and branches. Over time, as its process, its failure to hit its goal, is repeated, satisfaction attains to this repetition and the prior object, the lost object of desire, is abandoned. For example, some theorists today find the analytic category of the subject theoretically uninteresting, essentially useless; they've turned instead to objects, locating there new kinds of agency, vitality, and even politics.

The recent reactivation of communism also bears witness to the end of melancholia as a structure of left desire. Describing the massive outpouring of enthusiasm for the 2009 London conference on the idea of communism, Costas Douzinas and Slavoj Žižek note that the question and answer sessions were "good-humored and non-sectarian," a clear indication "that the period of guilt is over."[24] Even more pronounced is the movement against capitalism at work in 2011's Arab spring, European summer, and US fall. Globally, occupations put to work an insistent collectivity that struggles toward a new assertion of the common and commons.

24   Costas Douzinas and Slavoj Žižek, "Introduction: The Idea of Communism," in *The Idea of Communism*, ed. Costas Douzinas and Slavoj Žižek, London: Verso, 2010, ix.

Is it possible to understand this reactivation of communism in terms of desire, and if so, in what sense? I think that it is. In the next section, I defend two theses: first, communist desire designates the subjectification of the gap necessary for politics, the division within the people; second, this subjectification is collective—our desire and our collective desire for us.

The contemporary rethinking of communism provides at least two paths toward a concept of communist desire: the desire of the multitude and the desire of the philosopher. The first comes from Antonio Negri's Spinoza- and Deleuze-inspired emphasis on the productive desire of the multitude of singularities. Negri emphasizes that "the multitude is a totality of desires and trajectories of resistance, struggle, and constituent power."[25] The second, the desire of the philosopher (an expression provided by Alessandro Russo), tags Badiou's emphasis on the eternity of communism.[26] In a text from 1991, Badiou argues that the so-called

25   Antonio Negri, "Communism: Some Thoughts on the Concept and Practice," in *The Idea of Communism*, 163.
26   Alessandro Russo, "Did the Cultural Revolution End Communism?," in *The Idea of Communism*, 190.

death of communism wasn't an event. The political sequence associated with October 1917 had already long been dead. Communism as a political truth names an eternity, not an historical state formation, so it can't die—it necessarily exceeds any particular instantiation.[27] Badiou gives further expression to the philosophical idea of an eternal communism with his "communist invariants"—"the egalitarian passion, the Idea of justice, the will to end the compromises with the service of goods, the eradication of egoism, the intolerance towards oppression, the desire for the cessation of the State."[28] So, to reiterate, there is Negri who writes, "Communism is possible because it already exists in this transition, not as an end, but as a condition; it is the development of singularities,

27   Badiou writes, "'Communism,' having named this eternity, cannot anymore adequately name a death." See his *Of an Obscure Disaster*, trans. Barbara Fulks, Alberto Toscano, Nina Power, and Ozren Pupovac, Maastricht, NL: Jan van Eyck Academie, 2009, 19.
28   Ibid., 17. Bruno Bosteels emphasizes that these invariants are "the work of the masses in a broad sense" and "the immediate popular substance of all great revolts." See his *Badiou and Politics*, Durham, NC: Duke University Press, 2011, 277–278.

the experimentation of this construction and—in the constant wave of power relations—its tension, tendency, and metamorphosis."[29] And there is Badiou who treats communism as a transhistorical truth, a regulative ideal capable of grounding (Badiou uses the word "incorporating") a subject in history. In one version, communism is already immanent in the world. In the other, communism is the real of a truth that introduces the impossible into the world.

These two seemingly opposed approaches to communist desire operate similarly. Each points to an underlying communist necessity. Whether as the real existing power of the multitude or the real of a truth procedure in the symbolic narrative of history (via an individual subjectification), communist desire is a given. What Negri positions within the totality of capitalist production in the present, Badiou positions within the eternity of the philosophical idea.

Negri and Badiou are reassuring. For those committed to egalitarian universalism and unwilling to accommodate themselves to the era's dominant capitalist realism, Negri and Badiou establish places to

29   Negri, "Communism: Some Thoughts on the Concept and Practice," 163.

stand, sites from which to think and act and understand thinking and acting. As communism, socialism,
the working class, and the social welfare state have all
been vilified and dismantled as utopian ideals and as
post-war compromise, this reassurance has been essential to the maintenance of courage, confidence, and
even knowledge of revolutionary theory and practice.[30]
At the same time, as Brown's discussion highlights,
such reassurance can and sometimes does become an
object of fetishistic attachment. It provides a guarantee
as if the time for guarantees had not passed, something
to hold onto in a setting of absence, a setting where loss
itself operates as a force.

The reassuring promise from Negri is that communism has already arrived; it needs only to be released
from its capitalist constraints. Rather than a political-
economic system ruptured by division and antagonism,
one where the desires and activities of producers conflict with themselves and with each other, the desire
of the multitude appears as an already given convergence, abundance, and wholeness, shielding us from

30 See Darin Barney's discussion of courage in "Eat Your
Vegetables: Courage and the Possibility of Politics," *Theory &
Event* 14, 2, 2011.

confrontation with the gap within and between us. The reassurance from Badiou is not only that there are truths, but that these truths are from time to time incorporated in the world. The implicit promise is then that the political truth of the idea of communism will again be incorporated in new subjects. Rather than a conviction forcing the divisions of enactment by a party and a state, the desire of the philosopher appears as a form of thought that may guide or direct the affective attachments of those who contemplate it. Rather than a ruptured field of practical and theoretical knowledge and will, this desire manifests itself as a form that sees and impresses itself on history's varying rebellious subjectivities.[31]

These approaches to communist desire (particularly in the reductive descriptions I've provided here) rub uneasily against the grain of the last thirty years or so of critical theory, especially against those strands of post-structuralist and postcolonial theory to which Brown gestures in her essay. While the refusal to give way on desire and wallow in melancholia is vital to the power of these approaches, something can nonetheless

31   See Bosteels, *Badiou and Politics*, 277.

be learned from those who compromised. First, not
all political struggles present or past are communist
(just as, *contra* Rancière, not all political struggles are
democratic). The subsumption of all *ongoing* political
struggles into the multitude (even if the multitude is
one of singularities) disavows the tensions and oppositions among them as well as the ways that these
tensions are and can be manipulated in the interests
of capital. The absorption of all *past* popular struggles
into a content unchanging over the course of millennia
discounts the impacts of prior struggles on later ones,
as well as the material and technological determinations of forces, capacities, and interests.[32] One doesn't
have to embrace the historicist's happy positivism to
argue that the communist combination of emancipation
and egalitarianism is unique. It is informed by multiple other struggles—as Marx already makes clear in
distinguishing, for example, between bourgeois and proletarian revolutions and as twentieth-century struggles
for civil and women's rights and twenty-first-century
struggles for gay and trans rights attest. But it is not
the same as these struggles. Second, and consequently,

32   I rely here on Bosteels, ibid., 278.

communism is informed by its own failures and mistakes—an informing repressed by reassuring appeals
to a communist entirety or invariance.[33] This is why
there is an endeavor to rethink communism today, to
critique and learn from the past in order to instantiate
something better this time. There are specific histories and struggles whose successes and failures can
continue to inspire, that can—but may not—incite a
desire to look at our present differently, to see it in light
of the communist horizon.[34]

Why disavow knowledge of the differences among
struggles beneath the expanse of an eternal communist
substance? If there was a left structure of desire appro-
priately understood as melancholic, and if that structure
no longer holds, then some sort of working through has
taken place. Such work would have already called into
question all-encompassing visions of a communism
persisting apart from rather than through centuries of

33 My view here is informed by conversations with James
Martel as well as by his compelling argument in *Textual
Conspiracies*, Ann Arbor, MI: University of Michigan Press,
2011, 147–149.
34 See also Bosteels' dialectical approach to "concrete
history and the ahistorical kernel of emancipatory politics,"
The Actuality of Communism, 275–283.

be learned from those who compromised. First, not all political struggles present or past are communist (just as, *contra* Rancière, not all political struggles are democratic). The subsumption of all *ongoing* political struggles into the multitude (even if the multitude is one of singularities) disavows the tensions and oppositions among them as well as the ways that these tensions are and can be manipulated in the interests of capital. The absorption of all *past* popular struggles into a content unchanging over the course of millennia discounts the impacts of prior struggles on later ones, as well as the material and technological determinations of forces, capacities, and interests.[32] One doesn't have to embrace the historicist's happy positivism to argue that the communist combination of emancipation and egalitarianism is unique. It is informed by multiple other struggles—as Marx already makes clear in distinguishing, for example, between bourgeois and proletarian revolutions and as twentieth-century struggles for civil and women's rights and twenty-first-century struggles for gay and trans rights attest. But it is not the same as these struggles. Second, and consequently,

32   I rely here on Bosteels, ibid., 278.

What's left? A new, shifted desire, one that recognizes the impossibility of reaching or achieving its object and holds on, refusing to cede it.[37] Žižek links this new desire to Lacan's notion of the "desire of the analyst."[38] Such a desire is collective, sustaining a community even as it has moved past the need for some kind of phantasmic support. Collectivity, built around a lack, provides a common desire capable of breaking through the self-enclosed circuit of drive without reinstalling a new authority or certainty.[39]

Even as they take communist desire as a kind of given, Negri and Badiou contribute to this other thinking of communist desire, one that, with Lacan, associates desire with the constitutive role of lack. Desire depends on a gap, a question, a missingness, and an irreducible non-satisfaction. In this vein (and in contrast to his usual approach to desire), Negri writes, "communist imagination is exalted in the moment of

37 Martel develops this idea via a reading of Poe's metaphor of the maelstrom.
38 Slavoj Žižek, *The Ticklish Subject*, London: Verso, 1999, 296.
39 That is, without reverting to what Martel theorizes as idolatry.

rupture."[40] Badiou, too, albeit differently, emphasizes rupture, the rupture of the event "in the normal order of bodies and languages as it exists for any particular situation." Each thereby links communism to a gap or a break (although, again, they differ in their theorization of the time and place of such a gap). Badiou expresses it well in his early writing: a militant obstinacy, a certain subjective form, "has always and forever accompanied the great popular uprisings, not when they are captive and opaque (like everything we see today: nationalisms, market fascination, Mafiosi and demagogues, raised on a pedestal of parliamentarianism), but rather in free rupture with being-in-situation, or counted-being which keeps them in check."[41]

These emphases on rupture resonate with Rancière's emphasis on the division within politics between politics and the police.[42] For Rancière, politics is the clash of two heterogeneous processes—the process of the police and the process of equality. He views the police

40   Antonio Negri, "Communism: Some Thoughts on the Concept and Practice," 161.
41   Badiou, *Of an Obscure Disaster*, 6, 17–18.
42   See my discussion of Rancière in "Politics without Politics," *Parallax* 15:3, 2009.

DESIRE   189

as "an order of bodies that defines the allocation of
ways of doing, ways of being, and ways of saying...It
is an order of the visible and the sayable." He then
uses "politics" to designate "whatever breaks with the
tangible configuration whereby parties and parts or
lack of them are defined by a presupposition that, by
definition, has no place in that configuration—that of
the part of those who have no part."[43] Politics inscribes
a gap within an existing order of appearance. The "part
of those who have no part" is this gap in the existing
order of appearance between that order and other possible arrangements, this space between and within
worlds. The part-of-no-part doesn't designate a subset
of persons, a "we" or a "concrete identity" that can be
empirically indicated. It names the gap, division, or
antagonism that marks the non-identity of any ordering
with its own components. The Lacanian term for the
part-of-no-part would then be *objet petit a*, an impossible, formal object produced as the excess of a process
or relation, a kind of gap that incites or annoys, the
missingness or not-quite-rightness that calls out to us.
It's the gap, the mis- or non-identity between something

43 Jacques Rancière, *Disagreement*, trans. Julie Rose,
Minneapolis: University of Minnesota Press, 2004, 29–30.

simply present and something desired, the object-cause of desire or, returning to the political field, the gap between a politicized people and a population or set of persons.

Rancière notes that political subjectification is itself a disidentification and registration of a gap.[44] He explains: there are "political modes of subjectification only in the set or relationships that the *we* and the *name* maintain with the set of 'persons,' the concrete play of identities and alterities implicated in the demonstration and the worlds—common or separate—where these are defined."[45] So we have a rupture or a gap and the subjectification of this gap. But subjectification in what sense? There are different politicizations, different mobilizations and subjectifications that call out to and organize different convictions and interests.

The gap necessary for *communist* desire is manifest in the *non-coincidence* of communism with its setting, the gap that is within and part of the setting, as Marxist themes of negation and the communist legacy of revolution both affirm. Communism is of course not the only political ideology that mobilizes negation

44   Ibid., 36.
45   Ibid., 59.

and revolution—there are and have been liberal-democratic, bourgeois revolutions. And communism shares with capitalism a revolutionary mobilization of negation, hence communism as the negation of the negation. The difference in the ways they subjectify the gap, then, is crucial. Capitalist subjectification, the desire it structures and incites, is individual (even as it tends to sublimate desire in drive, or, differently put, even as individuated desires get caught up in and give way to drive's powerfully repetitive circuits). To invert Althusser, capitalism interpellates subjects as individuals. A communism that does likewise fails to effect a rupture or install a gap. Communist desire can only be collective, a common relation to a common condition of division.

Rancière's connecting of political subjectification to the gap between "we" and the set of persons points in this direction: it describes a common relation to a common condition of division that is subjectified as the "we" of a collective subject. Negri directly and explicitly emphasizes *collective* desire. Badiou, in his writing on the "death of communism," invokes a collective subject, albeit one that at the time of the collapse of the Soviet party-state "has been inoperative for more than twenty years." Badiou observes that "it was the phrase 'we communists,' a nominal precision added to 'we revolutionaries,' which in turn gave political and subjective force to this 'we' construed as an ultimate reference—the 'we' of the class, the 'we' proletarians, which was never articulated, but which every ideal community posited as its source as a historical axiom. Or in other words: we, faithful to the event of October 1917." Badiou tells us that such a sense of "we" informed his adolescent understanding of Sartre's phrase "Every anti-communist is a dog." "Because," Badiou explains, "every anti-communist thereby manifested his hatred towards the 'we,' his determination to exist solely within the limits of the possession of himself—which is always the possession of some properties or goods."[46] A constitutive component of the communist subjectification of the gap between what exists and what could be, between working and capitalist classes, between revolutionaries faithful to October 1917 and other political subjectifications is the opposition between a collective "we" and an individual determined in and by his singular self-possession. The communist subject is not

46   Badiou, *Of an Obscure Disaster*, 11–12.

an ensemble or assemblage of individuals but a force opposed to such an individualism and its attachments.

Badiou qualifies this view today. Even as he insists that "every truth procedure prescribes a Subject of this truth, a Subject who—even empirically—cannot be reduced to an individual," he nonetheless highlights the subjectification of individuals: "What is at issue is the possibility for any individual, defined as a mere human animal, and clearly distinct from any Subject, to decide to become part of a political truth procedure." The individual decides. Badiou construes this decision of the individual as an "incorporation" into the "body-of-truth." The individual materializes truth in the world; he or she serves as the site of the synthesis of politics, ideology, and history. Badiou writes: "We will say that an Idea is the possibility for an individual to understand that his or her participation in a singular political process (his or her entry into a body-of-truth) is also, in a certain way, a *historical* decision."[47] Describing a conversion markedly similar to the Christian's participation in the Holy Spirit, Badiou maintains:

47   Badiou, "The Idea of Communism," 2–3.

This is the moment when an individual declares
that he or she can go beyond the bounds (of selfish-
ness, competition, finitude ...) set by individualism
(or animality—they're one and the same thing). He
or she can do so to the extent that, while remaining
the individual that he or she is, he or she can also
become, through incorporation, an active part of a
new Subject. I call this decision, this will, a subjectivation. More generally speaking, a subjectivation
is always the process whereby an individual determines the place of a truth with respect to his or her
own vital existence and to the world in which this
existence is lived out.[48]

Insofar as Badiou argues that "communist" can no
longer "qualify a politics" or function as an adjective
for a party or a state, it makes sense that he has to find
another locus for communism's incorporation, that is,
for an operation capable of connecting truth to history.
Likewise, insofar as our contemporary setting is not one
wherein the story of the historical mission of the industrial working class to usher in communism remains
compelling, the question of the subject of communism is
open and pressing. Yet Badiou's choice of the individual

48   Ibid., 3.

as the locus of such a subject effaces the difference that matters in communist desire: it is and has to be collective, the common action and will of those who have undergone a certain proletarianization or destitution, of those who relinquish their attachment to an imaginary individuality. If communism means anything at all, it means collective action, determination, and will.

Under conditions of capitalism's cult of individualism, to emphasize acts of individual decision and will reduces communism to one among any number of possible choices. Such an emphasis thereby assents to capitalist form, rendering communism as just another content, an object of individual desire rather than the desire of a collective subject. In Badiou's version, the individual's active participation in a new subject doesn't even require any radical change on the part of the individual—he or she can remain "the individual that he or she is." What gets lost is the common that gives communism its force. This is the very loss that drives capitalism. Communism is subordinated to an individual's decision for it. Desire remains individual, not communist; nothing happens to its basic structure. In effect, desire is sublimated within the larger circuits of drive which perpetually offer different objects, different nuggets to enjoy, different opportunities to get off on failure, repetition, and the immediate movement from one thing to another. Social, economic, and political conditions may well contribute to a setting wherein the choice for communism becomes more compelling to more individuals, but the constitution of these individuals as something more, as a "we," has fallen out of the picture.

Although our political problem differs in a fundamental way from that of communists at the beginning of the twentieth century—we have to organize individuals; they had to organize masses—Georg Lukács's insight into individualism as a barrier to collective will-formation is crucial to theorizing communist desire as collective desire. Lukács notes that the "freedom" of those of us brought up under capitalism is "the freedom of the individual isolated by the fact of property," a freedom over and against other, isolated individuals, "a freedom of the egoist, of the man who cuts himself off from others, a freedom for which solidarity and community exist at best only as ineffectual 'regulative ideas.'" He writes, "The *conscious* desire for the realm of freedom can only mean consciously taking the steps that will really lead to it. And in the awareness that in contemporary bourgeois society individual freedom can only be corrupt and corrupting because it is a case of unilateral privilege based on the unfreedom of others, this desire must entail the renunciation of individual freedom."[49] Communist desire is a desire for collectivity.

In a setting of capitalism's distractions and compulsions, one may very well feel like something is wrong, something is missing, something is deeply unfair. Then one might complicate this idea, or contextualize it, or forget about it and check email. Or one might try to make a difference—signing petitions, blogging, voting, doing one's own part as an individual. And here is the problem: one continues to think and act individualistically. Under capitalist conditions, communist desire entails "the renunciation of individual freedom," the deliberate and practical subordination of self in and to a collective communist will. This subordination requires discipline, work, and organization. It is a process carried out over time and through collective struggle. Indeed, it is active collective struggle that changes and reshapes desire from its individual (and for Lukács, bourgeois and reified) form into a common, collective one.

49 Georg Lukács, *History and Class Consciousness*, trans. Rodney Livingstone, Cambridge, MA: MIT Press, 1985, 315.

The most renowned and compelling account of the role of revolutionary struggle in constituting communist desire, that is, in reforming individual interests into a collective one, of course comes from Lenin. Lenin constantly insists on struggling, testing, learning, developing, forging. The overthrow of the old society cannot occur without "prolonged effort and hard-won experience." In "'Left-Wing' Communism," Lenin presents a "fundamental law of revolution": "It is only when the *'lower classes' do not want* to live in the old way and the *'upper classes' cannot carry on in the old way* that the revolution can triumph." The lower classes have to want in a communist way. If they are to overthrow capitalism and begin establishing a communist society, they have to desire as communists. Without collective, communist desire, revolutionary upheaval moves in counterrevolutionary directions. Lenin writes, "A petty bourgeois driven to frenzy by the horrors of capitalism is a social phenomenon which, like anarchism, is characteristic of all capitalist countries. The instability of such revolutionism, its barrenness, and its tendency to turn rapidly into submission phantasms, and even a frenzied infatuation with one bourgeois fad or another—all this is common knowledge."[50] "Submission phantasms"—here Lenin designates a failure of collective will, a failure that seeks the cover of a master rather than holding fast to a communist desire to steer, with courage and without certainty, the conditions we are always ourselves already making.

In my account of communist desire, I've emphasized lack (the openness of desire) and its subjectification. I've argued that communist desire is the collective subjectification of an irreducible gap. Communist desire names the collective assumption of the division or antagonism constitutive of the political. Collectivity is the form of desire in two senses: our desire and *our desire for us*; or, communist desire is the collective desire for collective desiring.

Statistical identity provides a contemporary figure for such a desire. As I mentioned, Badiou links the communist invariants to great popular uprisings in free rupture with counted being. As he uses it in the context of his discussion of the "death of communism," the idea of counted being affiliates with a

50 V. I. Lenin, "'Left-Wing' Communism," in *The Lenin Anthology*, ed. Robert C. Tucker, New York: Norton, 1975, 554, 602, 559.

200 THE COMMUNIST HORIZON

larger critique of the State and Law, more particularly with the work of State and Law in ordering a situation and determining its facts. In a somewhat more literal criticism of counting as a mode of contemporary state power, Rancière criticizes polling as a rendering of the people as "identical to the sum of its parts," as nothing but its demographic components.[51] Rather than agree with Badiou and Rancière, I suggest a counter-thesis: a count can provide a form for expressing collectivity, even for rupturing the very setting in which it arises.

One of the slogans to emerge with particular power out of the movement to Occupy Wall Street is "We are the 99%." Instead of naming an identity, the number highlights a division and a gap, the gap between the wealth of the top 1 percent and the rest of us. As it mobilizes the gap between the 1 percent owning half the country's wealth and the other 99 percent of the population, the slogan asserts a collective and a common. It does not unify this collectivity under a sub-stantial identity—race, ethnicity, nationality. It asserts it as the "we" of a divided people, the people divided between expropriators and expropriated. In the setting

51   Rancière, *Disagreement*, 105.

of an occupied Wall Street, this "we" is a class, one of two opposed and hostile classes, those who have and control the common wealth, and those who do not. The announcement that "We are the 99%" names an appropriation, a wrong. In so doing, it also voices a collective desire for equality and justice, for a change in the conditions through which the 1 percent seizes the bulk of what is common for themselves, leaving the 99 percent with the remainder.

Additionally, "We are the 99%" erases the multiplicity of individuated, partial, and divided interests that fragment and weaken the people. The count dis-individualizes interest and desire, reformatting both within a common. Against capital's constant attempts to pulverize and decompose the collective people, the claim of the 99 percent responds with the force of a belonging that not only cannot be erased but that capital's own methods of accounting produce: *Oh, demographers and statisticians! What have you unleashed? As capital demolishes all previous social ties, the counting on which it depends provides a new figure of belonging!* Capital has to measure itself, count its profits, its rate of profit, its share of profit, its capacity to leverage its profit, its confidence or anxiety in its capacity for future profit. Capital counts and analyzes who has what, representing to itself the measures of its success. These very numbers can be—and in the slogan "We are the 99%" they are—put to use. They aren't resignified—they are claimed as the subjectification of the gap separating the top 1 percent from the rest of us. With this claim, the gap becomes a vehicle for the expression of communist desire, that is, for a politics that asserts the people as a divisive force in the interest of overturning present society and making a new one anchored in collectivity and the common.

In a close engagement with Catherine Malabou's discussion of severe brain injuries, Žižek discusses the logic of dialectical transitions: "After negation/alienation/loss, the subject 'returns to itself,' but this subject is not the same as the substance that underwent the alienation—it is constituted in the very movement of returning to itself."[52] Žižek concludes, "*the subject is* as such *the survivor of its own death*, a shell which remains after it is deprived of its substance." Proletarianization is a name for the process of this deprivation under capital. The deprivation of substance—common, social

52   Žižek, *Living in the End Times*, 307.

substance—leaves collectivity as its shell, as the form that remains for communist desire.

This collective form overlaps with the object-cause of communist desire, the people understood as the part-of-no-part. As I argue above, the part-of-no-part names the gap or antagonism that marks the non-identity of any ordering with its own components. It can thus be designated with Lacan's *objet petit a*, an impossible formal object produced as the excess of a process, a missingness or off-ness that calls out to us. Žižek notes that for Lacan, the object of desire always remains at a distance from the subject; no matter how close the subject gets to the object, the object remains elusive.[53] The distinction between object and object-cause accounts for this difference; there is a gap because the object-cause is not the same as any old object to which it attaches. The object-cause is what makes an object desireable, not a property inhering in the object.

One might think that the object of communist desire would be a world without exploitation; a world characterized by equality, justice, freedom, and the absence of oppression; a world where production is common,

53   Ibid., 303.

distribution is based on need, and decisions realize the
general will. Once one starts to describe this perfect
world, though, it always comes up lacking. Something is
always missing—what about an end to sexism, racism,
and egoism? What about an end to social hierarchies?
What about religious freedom and the intolerant? What
about meanness and bullying? It's no surprise that communism's critics (at least as early as Aristotle in *The
Politics*) criticize communism as utopian and impossible. It seems another word for perfect. But the impossible
of communist desire is not the same as its cause. The
object-cause of communist desire is the people and,
again, the people not as a name for the social whole but
as a name for the exploited, producing majority.

For any government, system, organization, or
movement, the people remain elusive, incompatible with and disruptive of that which attempts to
reduce, constrain, or represent it. Authoritarianism,
oligarchy, aristocracy, representative democracy, parliamentary democracy—none of these forms worries
too much about the disconnect between government
and people. But the disconnect, the gap, matters for
communism because communism is not only an association for governance, but also an organization of

production.[54] (The gap also matters for fascism, which tries to deal with it by essentializing the people via blood, soil, and the Leader and attempting to externalize and eliminate the remaining and unavoidable antagonism.) The people are elusive. They exceed their symbolic instantiation as well as the images and fantasies that try to fill the gap. Communist desire, a collective desire to desire communism, occupies and mobilizes this gap, recognizing its openness (that is, the impossibility of the people) and treating it as the movement of communism itself—in the words of Marx and Engels (*The German Ideology*): "We call communism the *real* movement which abolishes the present state of things."

I have set communist desire in the space marked by the end of left melancholia and by an alternative to the way of the drive. Whereas some view drive's sublimation as the way beyond a desire configured in terms of law and its transgression, the collective notion of desire that I present breaks from drive's repetitive circuits.

54   Alberto Toscano makes this point with particular power in his "The Politics of Abstraction," *The Idea of Communism*, 202.

As in the image offered us by Álvaro García Linera, desire describes a collective subject in the actuality of its movement with "expecting and desiring eyes set upon the communist horizon." Instead of being trapped in failure—and getting off on this failure—communist desire subjectifies its own impossibility, its constitutive openness. Such subjectification is inextricable from collective struggle, from the impact of changes over time that enable what James Martel calls the recognition of misrecognition, that is, the acknowledgement of false starts and errors, of fantasy constructions and myths of completeness and inevitability.[55] Because such struggle is necessarily collective, it forges a common desire out of individuated ones, replacing individual weakness with collective strength.

55   Martel, *Textual Conspiracies*.

Chapter Six

Occupation and the Party

The general horizon of our era is communist. Communism configures our setting, providing it with the shape that it takes. Communism is present as the force of an absence and an alternative, as the general field and division of the common, as the subjectification of the gap of desire. I conclude with a sixth feature that communism tags—the party. Whereas current dismissals of the party form proceed as if the very notion of the party depends on the fantasy that the party can know and realize the people's desire, I argue that the party is a vehicle for maintaining a specific gap of desire, the collective desire for collectivity.

Communism as the party returns to and overlaps with communism's most conventional referent—the Soviet Union. The communist party and the Soviet Union encounter the same criticisms: overly unified, hierarchical, exclusionary, and dogmatic. Insofar as communism tags both the USSR and a political party (that is, insofar as the two intermix and become indis-tinguishable), the left alternative to them has been formed out of opposition to both. It thus tends to be characterized by diversity, horizontality, individual-ity, inclusivity, and openness (where openness actually means the refusal of divisive ideological content). That these attributes also apply to the global networks of communicative capitalism, that they are celebrated by advertisers and invoked as best practices for efficient corporations, tends to be left unsaid. That exploitation and expropriation persist and can only be addressed through organized collective power is shunted aside, diverted around an individualist fantasy.

Consider David Graeber's contrast between "classi-cal sectarian Marxist groups" and "anarchist-inspired groups." Marxist groups, he writes, "invariably organ-ize around some master theoretician, who offers a comprehensive analysis of the world situation and, often, of human history as a whole, but very little theoretical reflection on more immediate questions of organization and practice." In contrast, anarchist-inspired groups generally "operate on the assumption that no one could, or probably should, ever convert another person completely to one's own point of view, that decision-making structures are ways of managing diversity, and therefore, that one should concentrate instead on maintaining egalitarian processes and considering immediate questions of action in the present." Graeber acknowledges that his distinction is rather stark, even misleadingly so. What he thinks is important, though, is the contrast between vanguardism, the leading role of intellectuals or a party, and what he positions as the alternative, namely, a consensus process "built on a principle of compromise and creativity where one is constantly changing proposals around until one can come up with something *everyone* can at least live with."[1]

The global movements of occupation and protest gathering political momentum in 2011 seem at first glance to be clear indications that the anarchists are right.[2] Occupy Wall Street emphasized consensus, inclusion, and the practices necessary to maintain and support occupation. It did without leaders, spokespersons,

1   David Graeber, "The Twilight of Vanguardism," *The World Social Forum: Challenging Empires*, June 2001, choike.org.
2   See the articles published as a special supplement to *Theory & Event* 14:4, 2011, ed. Jodi Dean, James Martel, and Davide Panagia.

and demands. The ideas of autonomy, horizontality, and leaderlessness that most galvanized people at the movement's outset, however, came later to be faulted for conflicts and disillusionment within the movement. Emphases on autonomy encouraged people to pursue multiple, separate, and even conflicting goals rather than work toward common ones. Celebration of horizontality heightened skepticism toward organizing structures like the General Assembly and the Spokes Council, ultimately leading to the dissolution of both. Assertions of leaderlessness as a principle incited a kind of paranoia around leaders who emerged but who could not be acknowledged or held accountable as leaders. So rather than solving the problem of left political organization by focusing on process and immediate questions of action, as anarchism suggests, Occupy Wall Street in fact poses it anew. It pushes us to think again about the role of a communist party.

On the flipside, just as Occupy can help us think about what a party might do or mean today, so does thinking about the party provide an alternative vision of the movement's strength as arising from its assertion of division, its new mode of representation, and its affirmation of collective power. With this understanding of its strengths, Occupy can temper autonomy with solidarity (recognizing that individualized autonomy can be a barrier to solidarity, that is, collective autonomy), add vertical and diagonal strength to the force of horizontality, and attune itself to the facts of leadership (leaders emerge and serve different purposes). It can provide the contours, in other words, for a new kind of communist party, one indistinct and in formation yet discernible in the gap of a collective desire for collectivity that the movement inscribes within the repetitive circuits of communicative capitalism.

September 2011 shattered the ideology of an invincible Wall Street much as September 2001 shattered the illusion of an invulnerable United States. All of a sudden and seemingly out of the blue, people outraged by the fact that "banks got bailed out" and "we got sold out" installed themselves in the financial heart of New York City. Occupying the symbol of capitalist class power, they ruptured it. The ostensible controllers of the global capitalist system, still reeling from the crash of 2008, appeared to have lost control over their own cement neighborhood. Hippies with tents and cops with barricades had turned Lower Manhattan into a chaotic mess. Those seeking to combine the people's work, debts, hopes, and futures into speculative instruments for private profit confronted a visible and actual collective counterforce. There in the power of the people where investment banks and hedge funds had already identified an enormous social surplus, a cadre of the newly active located an inexhaustible political potential. It was like a giant hole had been opened up in the steel and glass citadel of the financial class. Through it, traders, brokers, and market-makers—as well as *everybody else*—could see the possibility of a world without capitalism. Wall Street was occupied.

As it unfolded in New York City in the fall of 2011, occupation demonstrated itself to be more than a tactic. Occupy became an evental site and political form. I use the term "evental site" to point to the *event* of the movement, its rupturing of our political setting. Occupy Wall Street changed the US Left. Before Occupy, the Left was fragmented, melancholic, depressive. Now *we* appear to *ourselves*—we say "we," even as we argue over who we are and what we want. We say "we" knowing that there are divisions and differences among us that we express and that the term "we" expresses. Because of Occupy Wall Street, we have been able to imagine and enact a new subject that is collective, engaged, if, perhaps, also manic and distractible. Appearing differently to ourselves, seeing ourselves as changing the situation we are in, we also see our setting differently. It doesn't look like it did before—it's ruptured, open. Our setting is no longer fixed and given as the intractable reality of capitalism.

Badiou (writing about the Paris Commune) observes that a political rupture is always a combination of a subjective capacity and an organization of the consequences of that capacity.[3] The rupture brought about by Occupy combines the courage to manifest ourselves as a collective political presence (the subjective capacity) with the elimination (or inexistence) of the supposition that we will go along with the status quo, that we will stand by and do nothing as we are dispossessed of our lives and futures (the organization of the consequences of the subjective capacity). With Occupy, we have introduced a new political subject into the scene. This changes everything.

Thinking about Occupy Wall Street as an evental site allows for a certain repetition, reflexivity, or

3 Alain Badiou, *The Communist Hypothesis*, trans. David Macey and Steve Corcoran, London: Verso, 2010, 227.

self-inclusion. This reflexivity marks the event of the site as a subjectification, a forcing of a new being-thus. To paraphrase Badiou, Occupy "imposes itself on all the elements that bring about its existence."[4] Occupy is more than the sum of its parts. It's the parts and the sum. Those who resist attempts to represent the movement's politics and constituencies can be understood as voicing this "extra" dimension, the way the movement is an element of itself. A merely empirical description can't account for this excess over its elements that is the movement.

In addition to being an evental site, the movement around Occupy Wall Street is an organization of capacities and intensities, a political form for the incompatibility, the irreducible gap, between capitalism and the people. To conceive Occupy as a *political form* is to think of it as a configuration of opposition within a particular social-historical setting. To call Occupy a political form for *the incompatibility between capitalism and the people* is to say that it has a specific and fundamental content *and* that this content consists in the concentration of intensities around the gap of

4　Ibid., 208.

capitalism's failure as an economic system adequate to the capacities, needs, demands, and collective will of the people. On the one hand, this emphasis on the gap between capitalism and the people locates the truth of the movement in class struggle, in the antagonism between the exploiters and the exploited, those who own and those who do not, the rich and the rest of us. On the other, the emphasis on the gap between capitalism and the people marks the change in the setting of class struggle, a difference in setting such that to refer to the two great hostile classes as the proletariat and the bourgeoisie is no longer as obvious and compelling as it once was. It now appears as if everything is capitalism and this makes capital appear in its communicative, social, and affective—that is to say its *common*—dimensions.

How, then, does Occupy configure opposition within its—within our—setting? As I explained in chapter four, our setting is one of the convergence of communication and capitalism in a formation that incites engagement and participation in order to capture them in the affective networks of mass personalized media. These networks materialize a contradiction. They produce a common, a collective information and communication mesh of circulating affects and ideas. Yet these networks also presuppose and entrench individualism such that widely shared ideas and concerns are conceived less in terms of a self-conscious collective than they are as viruses, mobs, trends, moments, and swarms, as if collectivity were nothing but an object of epidemiology (an idea or image with an impact "goes viral"). The *event* of Occupy, Occupy's capacity to intervene in our setting, making it and us different from what we were before, has to be understood in terms *not of continuity* with communicative capitalism but of rupture, of a hole or break. If Occupy simply continued to offer networks, brands, and individual choices, it would be indistinguishable from what we have. Indistinguishable, it would be incapable of making new possibilities appear. It would lack a subjective capacity.

Remarkably, even as Occupy uses communicative capitalism's networks and screens, its energy comes from a vanguard of disciplined, committed activists undertaking and supporting actions in the streets. The physical amassing of people outside produced a new sense on the US Left that collective resistance was again possible here. Protesters deliberately and openly abandoned the script of anodyne marches, adopting instead the new, demanding, and unceasing practice of occupation. *They chose inconvenience* in a society ideologically committed to it.

Not all protesters affiliated with a specific occupation occupied all the time. Some would sleep at the site and then go to their day jobs or schools. Others would sleep elsewhere and occupy during the day and evening. Still others would come for the frequent, hours-long General Assemblies. Nonetheless, occupation involved people completely—as Lukács would say, *"with the whole of their personality."* As the occupations persisted over weeks and months, people joined in different capacities—facilitation, legal, technology, media, medical, food, community relations, education, direct action—participating in time-intensive working groups and support activities that involved them in the movement even as they weren't occupying a space directly. The movement became "a world of activity for every one of its members."[5]

The dedicated vanguard that is Occupy ruptured the

5   Georg Lukács, *History and Class Consciousness*, trans. Rodney Livingstone, Cambridge, MA: MIT Press, 1985, 335, 227.

lie that "what's good for Wall Street is good for Main Street." Occupy claims the division between Wall Street and Main Street and names this division a fundamental wrong, the wrong of inequality, exploitation, and theft. I turn, then, to division as the first of three key features of Occupy that account for its specific configuration of opposition and concentration of intensities and point toward new possibilities for the party form.

Occupy Wall Street asserts the incompatibility between capitalism and the people. Its central slogan, "We are the 99%," transforms a statistic into a crime. It subjectifies it. The slogan takes an empirical fact regarding a numerical determination of the 1 percent's degree of prosperity relative to that of the 99 percent and *politicizes* this fact, separating it out from the information stream as a fact that *matters*, that is more than simply one among many innumerable facts. We can contrast this slogan with those of Barack Obama's 2008 presidential campaign: "Change We Can Believe In" and "Yes We Can." Filled in by his emphasis on unity, on coming together in "a more perfect union," these slogans obscure division, attempting to repress and depoliticize it.

Occupy cut a hole in this ideological image of unity and made the underlying division appear. Politicians lamented the turn to class warfare—but they haven't denied it. The 1 percent complained that they shouldn't be hated for being rich—but they haven't denied the fundamental inequality. As a Pew Research Center poll found, 66 percent of Americans think that divisions between rich and poor are strong or very strong, an increase of 19 percent since 2009. Not only is this view held in every demographic category, but more people think that class division is the principal social division than they do any other division.[6]

Some in the movement have missed the point of Occupy's forcing of division, as if the movement were nothing but an extension of the hope and change promised by the Obama campaign. Rather than emphasizing class struggle, they emphasize the multiplicity of the 99 percent's incompatible groups and tendencies, and democracy as a process of integrating them. On this view, Occupy serves as a kind of political or even post-political open-source brand that anyone can

6 Rich Morin, "Rising Share of Americans See Conflict Between Rich and Poor," Pew Research Center, January 11, 2012, pewsocialtrends.org.

use. Because occupation is a tactic that galvanizes
enthusiasm ("tactics as brand"), it can affectively and
democratically connect a range of incompatible political positions, basically working around fundamental
gaps, divisions, and differences.

There are two mistakes here: first, ignoring the antagonism that connects the movement to its setting, namely,
class struggle as a contemporary struggle against proletarianization; and second, effacing the distinction
between Occupy and the elements that bring about its
existence. By denying the fundamental opposition to
Wall Street that divides the movement from the politics
that preceded it, the embrace of multiplicity proceeds
as if we were just the same assortment of individuals
with opinions and views as before, rather than a collectivity so threatening as to incite overwhelming and
violent police response. As a consequence, participants
are encouraged to emphasize their individual positions
rather than cultivate a general, collective one. The
result is that they continuously confront one another's
particularities as differences that must be expressed
rather than, say, disciplined, repressed, redirected,
sacrificed, or ignored as not relevant for this struggle.

"Tactics as brand" neglects the way occupation is a

form that organizes the incompatibility of capitalism with the people, its direct and material establishment of a physical base where people persist in bodily opposition to capital. As Naomi Klein points out in a contrast with the event-oriented alter-globalization movement, occupation establishes a fixed political site as a base for operations.[7] Holding a space for an indeterminate amount of time breaks with the transience of communicative capitalism, allowing a more durable politics to emerge. While the encampments were active, people had the opportunity to be more than spectators. After learning of an occupation, they could join. The protest wasn't over. Occupation implies a kind of permanence: people are in it till "this thing is done"—until the basic practices of society, of the world, have been remade. To be sure, this benefit is also a drawback. Since occupations are neither economically self-sustaining nor chosen tactically as sites from which to expand on the ground (block by block, say, until a city is taken), there is a problem of scale built into their form. But rather than addressing this problem of scale, "tactics

7 Naomi Klein, "Occupy Wall Street: The Most Important Thing in the World Now," *The Nation*, October 6, 2011, thenation.com.

as brand" sidesteps it by treating "occupation" as an easily replicable set of practices (when occupation is actually difficult and demanding!).

"Tactics as brand" highlights flexibility and adaptability, and in so doing makes occupation fully compatible with capitalism. Reduced to "tactics as brand" or "tactics as generator of affective attachment," Occupy Wall Street isn't a new political subjectification at all. It's a platform anyone can use if they feel like it. From this perspective, Occupy is just another strand of informational and affective content that appears on our screens and is intensely felt before other images pop up; it's compatible with the system it ostensibly rejects.

Similar problems hold for the emphases on plurality and inclusivity also prevalent in movement rhetoric. They merge seamlessly into communicative capitalism and thereby efface the class antagonism at the movement's heart, as if the movement were but a physical internet where people can post and blog and rant and opine without having to live with and adapt to the opacities of others for the sake of a common interest. It's already the case that there are multiple ideas and opportunities circulating on the internet—so the contribution of the movement isn't its ability to provide them. It's already the case that people can hold events, form digital groups, and carry out discussions. People can even assemble in tents on sidewalks—as long as they are in line for movie tickets or a big sale at Wal-Mart.

Communicative capitalism is an open, mutable field. It's inclusive, all-encompassing, mobile, and malleable. That aspect of the movement—inclusivity—isn't new or different. It's a component of Occupy that is *fully compatible* with the movement's setting in communicative capitalism. What's new (at least in the last thirty years) is the *organized collective opposition to the capitalist expropriation of our lives and futures* (and I should add here that this *organized collective opposition* —even in its still frustratingly inchoate and fragile current form—also marks the difference between the event of the movement and our prior time of assorted small socialist and communist parties, some of which supported Obama and others of which have been reluctant to work as a popular front; before Occupy they had lost whatever capacity they might have once had to enable the collective forcing of opposition to capitalism; it remains to be seen whether they will adapt). In the face of the multiple evictions and massive police response to the occupations, Occupy faces the challenge of keeping present and real the gap, the incompatibility, between occupation and the ordinary media practices and individualized acts of resistance that already comprise the faux-opposition encouraged in everyday life.

Keeping division from being absorbed in communicative capitalism is hard. Capitalist society is already divided, with multiple gaps, omissions, and glitches. Occupy Wall Street, then, does more than divide. It forcibly inscribes division. Occupy asserts division *and* this asserting makes division more than itself; it makes it itself plus its assertion. Without this forcible inscription of division, division would be nothing but forking and splitting and hence fully compatible with communicative capitalism. Pointing toward new ways of thinking about the work of the party, Occupy Wall Street reinvents representation as the active, self-authorizing assertion of division in relation to the appearing of antagonism. In Occupy's new politics of representation, division isn't effaced, displaced, or overcome. It's asserted and linked to capitalism's fundamental antagonism: class struggle.

Some argue that Occupy completely breaks with representation and representational politics.[8] There are two interconnected versions of this point. One emphasizes the individual subjects participating in the movement. The other emphasizes the movement's relation to its setting, to those outside it. The first rejection of representation holds that no one can or should speak for another person because doing so deprives the "spoken for" of their autonomy. According to this view, delegated autonomy is not autonomy at all but subjection to the opinion, will, and decision of another (as if collective action and common struggle were nothing but aggregation without submission, constraint, or transformation). Hence, to respect the autonomy of each, those in the movement have been encouraged to participate only in those actions with which they agree and to recognize that multiple heterogeneous processes comprise the movement; that these reflect conflicting, incompatible interests is pushed aside, repressed, only to return later with a vengeance. The second rejection of representation extends the first by insisting

8   For a discussion of this claim, see Jodi Dean and Jason Jones, "Occupy Wall Street and the Politics of Representation," *Chto Delat* 10:34, 2012.

that just as no one can speak for another, no one can speak for the movement. The movement is leaderless. Because Occupy is the multiplicity of the ever-changing people and practices comprising it, any attempt to represent the movement would necessarily restrict, judge, and negate it, reducing its potential to the already given terms and expectations of the dominant system. To proceed otherwise, it is claimed, elevates some voices and concerns over others, reinstating the hierarchies the movement works to dismantle. Not surprisingly, the fact that some voices and concerns do emerge as leaders, as dominant or more popular, induces in some participants a kind of insecurity and paranoia over the doublethink—*why are we all saying that this movement is completely horizontal when it's obviously not?*

The rejections of representation are misplaced. Treatments of Occupy as post- or anti-representational disavow division and thereby miss the new form of political representation Occupy is inventing. Those urging that each speak only for him- or herself disavow division *within* persons. Assuming that an individual can clearly know and represent her own interests, they avoid confronting the ways subjects are internally divided, not fully conscious of the desires and drives that motivate them. Furthermore, to the extent that they position the individual as the primary site and ground of political decisions, those arguing against representation fail to acknowledge how subjects are configured under capitalism. Speaking a liberal language of autonomy and a capitalist language of choice, they neglect the biases, misconceptions, and attachments structuring individual subjects. It's almost as if they fail to get their own critique, stopping it too soon. If representation excludes and hierarchizes, then these processes occur within persons as well as between them (an insight found not only in psychoanalysis but also in countless discussions of subject formation, discipline, and normativity).

Those who insist on the unrepresentability of Occupy also disavow division *between* persons. Failing to take division seriously enough, they embrace a nearly populist presumption of organic social totality. Not surprisingly, the fact of hierarchy—whether born of skills, privilege, diligence, or contingency—necessarily and unavoidably comes up against claims of horizontality, disillusioning people perpetually suspicious of actual and potential leaders. It's no wonder that an ideology of leaderlessness breeds suspicion—there aren't clear and open ways to select and reject leaders. For newcomers, it seems mysterious, like a hidden elite controls everything behind the scenes. Similarly, fearful of excluding potential opportunities, some in Occupy tried early on to avoid confronting fundamental divisions within the movement. They advocated a focus on the immediate tasks of occupation. The effect, though, was to reduce division to forking (in other words, to sublimate it). People pursued their own projects, perpetually splitting according to their prior interests and expertise, repeating the patterns dominant in communicative capitalism and failing to keep open the hole in Wall Street even as they dug multiple little ones. The fantasy at work in the insistence on the unrepresentability of Occupy is a fantasy of multiplicity without antagonism, of difference without division.

The Occupy movement brings together different political tendencies, varying degrees of radicality, and multiple interests and concerns. But this does not mean that it moves beyond representation. On the contrary, this broadness points to the unavoidability of representation as well as to its constitutive openness and malleability. What actions fit with the movement, which ones to take, and how directly they link up are ongoing questions. Ever-changing plurality is the condition of representation, not its overcoming. Those who construe Occupy as post- and anti-representation misread plurality as the negative limit to representation when they should instead recognize plurality as representation's positive condition. Occupy Wall Street is not *actually* the movement of 99 percent of the population of the United States (or the world) against the top 1 percent. It is a movement mobilizing itself around an occupied Wall Street *in the name of* the 99 percent. Asserting a division in relation to the fundamental antagonism Occupy makes appear, it represents the wrong of the gap between the rich and the rest of us.

Critics of representation miss the way Occupy reinvents the politics of representation because their image of representation remains deeply tied to parliamentarianism. It's true that Occupy eschews mainstream electoral politics. It is also true that Occupy rejects the nested hierarchies that conventionally organize political associations. But neither of these facts eliminates representation. Rather, they point to a rejection of the current political and economic system because of its failure to represent adequately the people's will, a will that is itself divided and can only be represented divisively.

Lacan's account of separation can help make sense of the way Occupy represents division. Lacan describes separation as the overlapping of two lacks. As Žižek emphasizes in a reading of Hegelian de-alienation as separation, "when the subject encounters a lack in the Other, he responds with a prior lack, with his own lack."[9] In other words, the subject realizes that not only does he not know, but the Other doesn't know either. Each is lacking. My suggestion is that Occupy reformats representation as an assertion of the overlap of two lacks and thereby separates the movement from its setting. Broken into three steps: 1. Occupy encounters the lack in the big Other (that is, the incompatibility of capitalism with the people, the corresponding failure of liberal democracy precisely insofar as it is capitalism's political form, and the overall decline of symbolic efficiency characteristic of communicative capitalism). 2. Occupy responds by asserting its own lack, whether

9   See Slavoj Žižek, "The Most Sublime of Hysterics: Hegel with Lacan," trans. Rex Butler and Scott Stephens, lacan.com/zizlacan2.htm.

as precarity (debt, unemployment, foreclosure), non-knowledge (no one really knows what to do, how to create a functioning egalitarian system of production and distribution), or incompleteness (the movement isn't a whole or unity; it's composed of multiple, conflicting groups and interests). And, 3. Occupy names or represents the overlap of these two lacks. It imposes itself as the "extra dimension" of the self-conscious assertion of the overlap.

Occupy Wall Street combines anti-representational rhetoric with the intensity of acts of representation. Few want to be represented; many want to represent. Frequently, video and photographic images of the movement show people recording and transmitting —representing—the movement. Admittedly, some live-streaming actions online present their coverage as journalism. They vary with respect to whether they position themselves as citizen-journalist-activists or as objective reporters covering stories neglected in mainstream media. Others see their tweets, photos, videos, and updates as key components of their activism: through these media contributions they spread awareness of the movement, inform people of ongoing and upcoming actions, and actively increase turnout

for meetings and demonstrations. A third, more reflex-
ive aspect of these representational practices appears
insofar as the images and reports share in a common
name, in a common relation to an occupied Wall
Street: this aspect is the self-constitution of the movement as a conscious collective practice. Together, in
combination, the multiple streams and images refor-
mat the sense of what is possible through collective
action.

Who is it for? Who do we imagine watching the
streams and forwarding or remediating the images? To
the extent that the imaginary audience is "anybody" or
"everybody," we accept and repeat the expectations of
communicative capitalism, looking outside the movement for validation, and preoccupying ourselves with
media and means rather than division and ends. But
to the extent that *we* are the audience, that *we* are the
collectivity of those calling ourselves into being as a
new movement of the people in opposition to capital,
we enhance our courage and intensify our confidence
in the political form of Occupy.

The third relevant aspect of Occupy as an evental
site and political form is collectivity. Breaking with

dominant tendencies toward the specification of issues and identities, the movement combined voices so as to amplify their oppositional political force. As I've already suggested, it replaced the ease of MoveOn-style "clicktivism" with the demanding and time-consuming practice of supporting an occupation. No wonder occupiers have been a vanguard—they are dedicated, disciplined, and unifying through practice a dispersed political field. Occupy arranges the physical presence of large groups of people outside, in visible, urban spaces, in political actions authorized by neither capital nor the state but by the people's collective political will. The self-authorized practices of a politicized collective amplify specific contradictions in the current arrangement of the capitalist state such as the relation between public and private property (a relation manipulated and occluded in networked communications platforms) and the distinction between legal and illegal (for example, Occupy Wall Street oscillates between actions that challenge capitalist state power and appeals to the law to protect them as they carry out these actions). Bluntly put, Occupy does work that Lenin associates with a revolutionary party: establishing and maintaining a continuity of oppositional struggle that enables broader numbers of people to join in the movement.[10] It builds collectivity.

In communicative capitalism, people can be virtually present in all sorts of numerically large concentrations. Individuals can pass through many urban spaces with relatively little hassle (particularly if they adhere to class, race, and gender codes). Capital and the state *can* and *do* organize and facilitate the presence of large numbers of people in one site or another. Occupy—occupation as a tactic—self-consciously and deliberately recombines these components in a specifically political form that intervenes as a new political subjectification, one that opens up a new sense of collective power.

In his discussion of the Paris Commune as an event, Badiou describes how those who were inexistent were brought into "a politically maximal existence."[11] As what was inexistent comes to exist, another element ceases to exist. With Occupy Wall Street, the collective and self-conscious assertion of our collectivity destroys

10   V. I. Lenin, "What Is to Be Done?," in *The Lenin Anthology*, ed. Robert C. Tucker, New York: Norton, 1975, 76–77.
11   Badiou, *The Communist Hypothesis*, 221.

our prior political incapacity, our prior subjection to the terms and frame of communicative capitalism. Now we can and are right to say "we." The movement is the form that incites our courage and confidence in doing so. We don't have to retreat either to the political weakness of dispersed individuals against the force of capital and the state or to the ideological imaginary of unique, strong, and complete individuals autonomously creating their own destinies.

We shouldn't be afraid to acknowledge, though, the continuing mistrust of collectivity. Even as people feel their collective power *during* marches and demonstrations, *through* chants asserting their power ("the people, united, will never be defeated"; "we are the 99 percent"), and *in* the People's Mic consolidation of voices, there remains anxiety around hierarchy, non-transparency, leadership, delegation, institutionalization, and centralization. Perhaps sensing, fearing, and repressing their own and others' enjoyment (whether of power or submission), people don't quite trust each other as participants in common struggle. On the one hand, people carry an individual sense that they have to do it themselves (or at least know all the details of what's being done). They don't trust that others will do things the right way, their way; they don't see themselves and each other as solidarily connected. On the other hand, some of us at the same time displace this sense of getting things done onto others. We assume that someone else is doing it or knows what's happening. We say, "well, let's wait and see what happens," as if we were someone removed from or outside the movement, as if the movement were the actions of others. This is the flipside of the suspicion toward leaders—someone else is in charge. It's also a kind of delegation without delegation, or a delegation without representation insofar as it holds onto a fantasy of autonomy as it denies the emergence, function, and need for leaders (that it nevertheless unconsciously embraces).

In the US setting of overall mistrust of the political and economic system, too many on the Left have tended to believe that autonomy, fragmentation, and dispersion can substitute for solidarity. Consider, for example, the affective oscillation between the sense that the movement gets energy from large numbers of people amassed together in a central location and the sense that networks of local, specific, and often temporary practices and projects are *the* best model for the movement (rather than the setting in which we are beginning and on which we build). Similarly, there is anxiety over practices of inclusion and exclusion, real challenges regarding different capacities for expression and collaboration, as well as over different opportunities to meet, discuss, and participate. The very meetings that make some people feel like they are building a new world make others feel like they are wasting their time, spinning their wheels, and getting nothing accomplished.

What's the alternative? Trusting our desire for collectivity. This means acknowledging how autonomy is only ever a collective product, fragments are parts of ever larger wholes, and dispersion is but the flipside of concentration. We might think here in terms of a dynamic rather than an either/or: dispersed local actions matter; they are amplified when they are linked to a movement that can bring out huge numbers of people for massive events. And these massive events are more than just spectacles, more than momentary hints at the people's will, when they are strengthened by the specific achievements of specific, targeted campaigns. In many ways, this has already been a key component of Occupy. Yet, too much movement rhetoric denounces centralization and celebrates local-ity such that people lose confidence in anything but the local and the community-based.

Likewise, strong structures, structures that can grow, structures with duration, need vertical and diagonal components in addition to horizontal ones. Again, this has been obviously true in the movement, yet much of the rhetoric of Occupy celebrates only horizontality, treating verticality as a danger to be fought at every turn. Diagonality is basically neglected, which means we haven't put much energy into developing structures of accountability and recall.

Collective power isn't just coming together. It's sticking together. And sticking together requires a willingness to make sacrifices for the sake of others. Many are already doing this, yet the movement doesn't acknowledge it insofar as its language celebrates and valorizes autonomy over collectivity. Collectivity is present in the common language and common actions in the movement, but not to and for itself. It's some-times asserted, sometimes experienced. But it has to be collectively desired and collectively built—hence the need for a party.

In sum, the Occupy movement demonstrates why

something like a party is needed insofar as a party is an explicit assertion of collectivity, a structure of accountability, an acknowledgment of differential capacities, and a vehicle for solidarity. It also gives us a sense of the form such a party might take: a self-conscious assertion of the overlap of two gaps in the maintenance of collective desire.

Some depict the Leninist party as a spectre of horror, the remnant of the failed revolution the terrors of which must be avoided at all costs. In such a vision (which may not be concretely held by anyone but seems vaguely intuited by many), communism is reduced not simply to the actual (which is always necessarily ruptured, incomplete, irreducible to itself, and pregnant with the unrealized potentials of the past) but to the parody of one actuality, an actuality that has in fact changed over time and from different perspectives. Through this reduction (which is an ongoing process), actuality is displaced by an impossible figure, a figure so resolute as to be incapable of revolutionary change. Rigid, exclusive, dogmatic—it's hard to see how such a party could even function in a revolutionary situation much less ever attract members in the first place: how would it get people to show up, to march, to write and distribute newspapers, to put their lives on the line? How would it grow or spread?

In contrast, Lukács's account of the Leninist party suggests an organization formed as the subjectification of two lacks, the chaos of revolution and the non-knowledge of the party. [12] Lukács argues that Lenin's party presupposes the actuality of revolution. It's a political organization premised on the fact of revolution, on the fact that the terrain of politics is open and changing and that revolutions happen. Revolutions are not messianic events wherein long-awaited deities intervene in human affairs. They are results, conditions, and effects of politics wherein states are overthrown, dismantled, distributed, reconfigured, redirected. In the chaos of revolution, tendencies in one direction can suddenly move in a completely opposite direction. Because the revolutionary situation is characterized by unpredictability and upheaval, no iron laws of history provide a map or playbook that revolutionaries can follow to certain victory.

That revolution is actual means that decisions,

12   Georg Lukács, *Lenin: A Study on The Unity of His Thought*, trans. Nicholas Jacobs, London: Verso, 2009.

actions, and judgment cannot be perpetually deferred. When we take them, we are fully exposed to our lack of coverage in history, to the chaos of the revolutionary moment. We have to be confident that the revolutionary process will bring about new constellations, arrangements, skills, and convictions, that through it we will make something else, something we haven't yet imagined. For the Leninist party, to wait, to postpone until we are sure, until we know, is to fail now.

The actuality of revolution requires discipline and preparation, not because the communist party can accurately predict everything that will occur—it cannot—and not because it has an infallible theory—it does not. Its theory, like the conditions in which it is set, is open to rigorous criticism, testing, and revision. Discipline and preparation enable the party to adapt to circumstances rather than be completely molded or determined by them. The party has to be consistent and flexible because revolution is chaotic. The actuality of revolution is thus a condition of constitutive non-knowledge for which the party can prepare. It's a condition that demands response, if the party is to be accountable to the exploited and oppressed people, if it is to function as a communist party.

A communist party is necessary because neither capitalist dynamics nor mass spontaneity immanently produce a *proletarian* revolution that ends the exploitation and oppression of the people. A revolutionary period brings together and confuses multiple and changing groups and classes. Different spontaneous tendencies, degrees of class consciousness, and ideological persuasions converge. The Leninist party doesn't know what the people want. It's a form for dealing with the split in the people, their non-knowledge of what they, as a collectivity, desire. As Lukács writes, "If events had to be delayed until the proletariat entered the decisive struggles united and clear in its aims there would never be a revolutionary situation."[13] What the party knows is that such a lack of knowledge must not impede action because it cannot forestall the actuality of revolution. The party, then, is an organization situated at the overlap of two lacks, the openness of history as well as its own non-knowledge.

The communist party occupies this site and subjectifies it; it provides a form for political subjectivity as it works in "total solidarity with and support for all the

13   Ibid., 31.

oppressed and exploited within capitalist society."[14] This dedication requires constant interaction with the struggling, proletarianized people. Constant interaction installs a double dynamic in the party. On the one hand, it must be strictly disciplined. On the other, it must be flexible and responsive, capable of learning from and adapting to the ever-changing situation. As it learns from the struggling masses, the party provides a vehicle through which they can understand their actions and express their collective will, much as the psychoanalyst provides a means for the analysand to become conscious of her desire.[15]

One might object that my use of Lukács to present a view of the Leninist party as a form responsive to lack and contingency is selective at best. Such an objection could emphasize Lukács's claim that "because the party, on the basis of its knowledge of society in its totality, represents the interests of the whole proletariat (and in doing so mediates the interests of all the oppressed—the future of mankind), it must unite within it all the contradictions in which the tasks that

14 Ibid., 30.
15 Slavoj Žižek, *Revolution at the Gates*, London: Verso, 2002.

arise from the very heart of this social totality are expressed."[16] This objection misses its target: to unite contradictions is not to resolve them. The party doesn't resolve contradictions; it expresses them as contradictions. Leninist revolutionaries take on themselves the demands and conflicts of the revolution. They perform the revolutionary situation, in all its chaos and uncertainty. To this extent, the Leninist party cannot be a party that makes demands on the people; it is a party that makes present to the people the demands they are already making on themselves, but can't yet acknowledge.

There is occupation and there is its politicization. As organized opposition to capitalism, the political form of occupation inscribes a gap that makes antagonism appear and forces this inscription as the division between the 1 percent and the rest of us. Failing to recognize how the event of the movement breaks with its setting, some have been reluctant to acknowledge the force of division and thus resistant to the very politics it enables. They prefer to insist that Occupy

16 Lukács, *Lenin: A Study on The Unity of His Thought*, 34.

is nonpartisan, post-political. This imbues the movement with liberal and capitalist (Lukács and Lenin would say "bourgeois") elements because that is our default mode, our immediate way of thinking, doing, and responding. Underplaying the crisis of capitalism and overplaying the capacity for democracy to produce political change, voices in the movement try to deny the division they enact.

The role of the party is to insist on division. A party politicizes a part. The communist party politicizes the part that is not a part, claiming the gap constitutive of the people and subjectifying it as the collective desire for collectivity. Its task is not to fulfill or satisfy this desire (an impossibility), but to maintain it, to cultivate it as a desire. In our present setting, communicative capitalism attempts to absorb our political efforts into its circuits. Conforming to its terms seems natural, necessary, the only way to struggle: *we must engage in elections; our actions must provide good media content; we need a catch phrase that will go viral.* This is movement as commodity and fashion choice. The party provides a form for resisting these terms, the false choice of compromise or nothing (inexistence, failure, irrelevance) that has resulted in left-wing melancholia.

As the organization of lack, it lets the choice for a gap be the choice for the power of collective desire.

Only by reading Occupy Wall Street through an insistence on the gap of desire, that is to say, in terms of the communist party as a form, is the communist horizon of the movement visible. To what crime does the movement respond? To which processes does it react? The remarkable rupture the movement effects arises out of its organization of a radical collective response to capitalism. Reading the movement any other way resubmerges it in what was already circulating through, and as individual contributions to, the affective networks of communicative capitalism.

But what do they want? What do you want? The question of demands infused the initial weeks and months of Occupy Wall Street with the endless opening of desire. Nearly unbearable, the lack of demands concentrated interest, fear, expectation, and hope in the movement. In these moments, the occupation functioned as a gap hystericizing the mainstream media, perhaps even the public it called into being. *What does the movement want—from us?! What is it demanding—of us?!* Occupy Wall Street was an other that reawakened political desire, forcing people to acknowledge the ways their compromised choice for liberal democracy and neoliberal capitalism has sublimated and betrayed their desire ... *and for what? For widespread proletarianization, global warming, and economic collapse?*

Contemporary communists are tasked with organizing individuals. (To be sure, Lukács grappled with capitalist over-individualization already in the twenties.) Those of us in the US, UK, and EU operate within an ideological setting that celebrates the individual, its unique voice and valuable opinion. Collectivity is either configured as stifling and oppressive or romanticized as the communitarian ground of authentic identity (whether ethnic, racial, religious, or otherwise). This ideological configuration displaces attention from the powerlessness of individuals *as individuals* to reform the systems determining their lives (systemic change requires the organized power of a group) to the wide range of opportunities for individual consumption and self-expression. It holds out these opportunities as a kind of lure or reward, as that special *something* collectivity threatens to take or abolish, obscuring the fact that for the vast majority such opportunities are there only as possibilities under threat, not actual experiences of freedom.

What do they want? What do you want? The party
seems poised to steal our enjoyment, making our individual voices and choices (and potential for fame and
wealth) all the more likely but for the threat to them.
Yet the question of what the party wants or the anxiety
so many on the Left have with regard to the party
exhibits the same transferential inversion at work in
the demand for demands addressed to Occupy Wall
Street—*what does the party demand of me?*—as if the
party would tell us what to do, what to want. Perhaps
the underlying desire is for a party that *could* tell us
what we want and how to get it. The operative fantasy is
that the party *really does* know how to organize society.
Or perhaps the underlying desire is for a party that
could force us to do what we secretly want and that
would give us the permission and means we need to
enjoy. We can smite our enemies, take all their stuff,
and be on the right (left) side of history! Leftists are
justifiably anxious with regard to the party—a desire
for collectivity is not the only desire for which parties
have provided a form. They have also served as forms
for desires for a master. Nonetheless, proceeding as
if the party is and can be only the form of a master
leaving the master's power in place, allowing it to

thwart our collective power all the more effectively.

The fantasies of a master help us avoid the more unbearable confrontation with the gap constitutive of the people. Together with the nuggets of momentary enjoyment we accrue in the repetitive circuits of capitalist drive, they defend us against a desire for collectivity that we don't yet want. Collectivity—common cause and common determination—is difficult. It involves giving up what we don't have for something we can't achieve. We are and cannot name a whole. We are and cannot fully justify the coercive and productive forces we unleash. The communist party is a form for maintaining this gap without yielding to fantasy or fatalism—which is why Badiou theorizes its operation in terms of courage as well confidence.[17] Neither instantiation nor representative of the people, the party formalizes its collective desire for collectivity; when the party fails to keep open the gap of desire, it ceases to be a communist party.

A couple of months after the movement to Occupy Wall Street was underway, a common gloss to the complaint

17 Alain Badiou, *Theory of the Subject*, trans. Bruno Bosteels, New York: Continuum, 2009, 330.

that the movement hadn't made any demands circulated. Its basic message was that the complaint was disingenuous. We know full well that the demand is for an end to the inequality and unfairness permeating the system. One of the images accompanying the message was of a mass—the people, the 99 percent— against one, *a fat cat high net worth individual* with a dollar sign on his suit. The goal of communism is also clear: from each according to ability, to each according to need. How we make this happen is up to us—it's the purpose and principle of the sovereignty of the people.